The Sales Professional

The Sales Professional

The Sales Professional

Joe Denham

BUSINESS
BOOKS

London, UK
Washington, DC, USA

CollectiveInk

First published by Business Books, 2025
Business Books is an imprint of Collective Ink Ltd.,
Unit 11, Shepperton House, 89 Shepperton Road, London, N1 3DF
office@collectiveink.com
www.collectiveink.com
www.collectiveinkbooks.com/business-books/

For distributor details and how to order please visit the 'Ordering' section on our website.

ISBN: 978 1 80341 779 0
978 1 80341 781 3 (ebook)
Library of Congress Control Number: 2024901692

A CIP catalogue record for this book is available from the British Library.

Design: Lapiz Digital Services

UK: Printed and bound by CPI Group (UK) Ltd, Croydon, CR0 4YY
Printed in North America by CPI GPS partners

We operate a distinctive and ethical publishing philosophy in all areas of our business, from our global network of authors to production and worldwide distribution.

To Lel. Could not have done it without you.

Acknowledgments

Blair and Grant Duncan, Graham Howton, Billy Spindloe, Nikki Thornton, Paul Sweetland, Paul Owen, Lesley, Ralph and Nora, Mum and Dad, My big brother Paul, Joey, Jack, Harley and Louis.

Contents

Section One — the Denham Method   1

Foreword   3

Preface   9

Introduction   11

1. What Does a Salesperson Do?   17
2. How Much Do You Want to Earn?   21
3. A Structured Approach: The Sales Cycle   23
4. Moving through the Sales Cycle   31
5. The Sales Pipeline   37
6. Secret Tools of a Salesperson   41
7. Features and Benefits   53
8. Maximising Your Time   57
9. Types of Meeting   61
10. Presentations   65
11. Forecasting and Reviewing   69
12. A Different Way to Set Targets   75
13. Territory and Customer Management   79
14. Electronic Data Interchange (EDI) Systems   87
15. Marketplace Selling   91
16. Social Media and the Advent of Retail Media   95
17. Be a Professional; You Don't Need Luck   101
18. The Denham Method: Summary   103

Section Two — Exporting (International Sales)   105

Section Three — Sales Tales   111

About the Author   127

Section One — the Denham Method

Foreword

I have worked with some incredible people over the years. Here's what a few of them had to say when I told them I was writing this book. You can scan their LinkedIn profiles after their comments.

James Allan, Global Sales Manager

I first met Joe at the National Hardware show in Las Vegas. At that time this was my first international trade show and Joe guided me during that time on how to effectively communicate and extract the required information from prospective buyers and the process in which to follow the lead up. A few months after meeting at the trade show I moved over from my last employer to work directly with Joe in international sales.

During this time Joe continued to mentor me through the sales cycle as well as how to deal with international buyers on a much higher level than I had done previously. Joe taught me how, through effective presentations as well as detailed and informative approaches to controlling meetings, we could ensure that we left with the desired results.

During my time working with Joe, he showed me the most efficient and timely way to travel to multiple locations around the world and how different cultures work from east to west. My sales career took off under Joe's guidance and I can recommend his sales methodology to any prospective salesperson. It works.

Nora Metaj, Online Sales Manager

In my journey in the world of sales, I have been fortunate to have the guidance and support of an exceptional mentor, Joe. His training methods have been instrumental in shaping my career and transforming me from a sales novice to a confident professional. What sets Joe apart is his steadfast commitment to honesty and integrity. He installed in me the importance of conducting business with transparency and sincerity, values that have not only made me a better salesperson but also a more trustworthy individual.

Joe's sales training is a testament to the belief that a strong work ethic can lead to unparalleled achievements. His steadfast dedication to excellence has shown me that with the right attitude and diligence, one can accomplish anything. It has inspired me to approach every task with a relentless determination to excel, knowing that hard work and dedication are the cornerstones of success. Another core lesson I have learnt is the art of controlling a meeting — a skill that has proved invaluable in my interactions with clients. Joe's sales training is meticulous and comprehensive, providing me with the tools and knowledge to confidently navigate complex sales conversations even with high-level individuals. I now find myself comfortably seated in meetings with influential clients and I attribute my success in the sales world to his enduring support and guidance. Moreover, Joe's guidance has not only helped me flourish in my career but also in my real life, as his principles of honesty and work ethic have had a positive impact beyond the office.

He has taught me a multitude of invaluable lessons, and while this is just a glimpse of what has moulded me into the person I am today, I want to express my heartfelt gratitude to Joe for his steadfast support and mentorship. In every success I experience, I will always look back to you, Joe, because you have imparted so much wisdom that I will carry with me throughout my life. Thank you for all you have done and for helping shape the individual I've become.

Blair Duncan, CEO

When I first met Joe in the early 90's, the Denham Method was yet to be branded as such, but it was there already, and working.

The concepts of Pipelines, Forecasts, the Sales Cycle, quality presentations, and having the right resources to both demonstrate and understand the client's buying cycle were clearly defined. The first time he told me, it became obvious. It wasn't obvious before then because no one had ever explained it that logically before.

We are talking of the days before Smartphones, when laptops were luggable and the Internet was not even in black and white yet, so the process was still mostly manual, using land lines. This meant you had to know not just where clients were in the cycle but also where they were physically, and that meant a continuous contact process and ensuring follow-ups were both timely and on time.

I accompanied Joe as the "Techie" to support him in calls for large, technical sales. It was easy, because not only were we confident we had the best product, but I also knew exactly what the client wanted and expected to see. That's because he ensured that the progression from a lead to a qualified prospect was consistent, detailed, and accurate. To this day I still have a notebook and a pen at every meeting I attend — online or in person. Our in-house CRM design is based on this methodology and has been for 30 years, and it still works because people buy from people.

You must be single-minded, self-motivated, and willing to guide the customer through the process until they realize that you really do have the best product, solution, or service — and that they want to buy it from YOU.

Now, it's smartphone based with AI supported CRM tools, but the basis and principles have never changed. People still buy from people. The Denham Method as described here is a logical process to take an introduction and get the order, and once consistently applied, you will get the order more often than not.

And while never explicitly stated, obviously, never ever drink more than 15 Suffering Bastards the night before a key presentation.

William Spindloe CHRM

I met Joe socially and after a fairly short period of time he told me there was a position in his company and he wanted to offer me the role. It was a sales role. Managing partners and selling direct to clients. I thanked him for his consideration, but I had never knowingly or deliberately sold anything to anyone. I came from a corporate training background. I had started working in the Middle East only 6 months prior. Not only had I not sold before, but this was a competitive multicultural territory, which added to the degree of difficulty. Joe asked me to spend the day with him as he felt he might provide me with a different perspective. This resulted in me joining a month later and being handed Oman as my first territory. A country I had visited once for a weekend.

I had joined three months into the financial year with the annual quota for the country hanging over me. I was initially concerned that maybe I had bitten off more than I could chew. Joe provided me with guidance on the management of the territory: choosing critical targets, finding the right person within the organisation, planning the approach, understanding the customers' goals and objectives, and structuring the conversation around how we could help them deliver. He also taught me to illustrate that working with us was an investment they had to make based around an incremental process. I exceeded the annual target in 8 months. The year after I became the top salesperson in the region and had the largest number of clients with around 80% on multi-year contracts.

On the day I spent with Joe prior to joining I asked him what made him think I could do this. He told me I was developing and delivering training and therefore effectively 'selling' ideas, strategies, and systems to rooms full of people all the time. He went on to say that we are all, in effect, selling. Whether it's in an interview for a new job or striving for promotion, it's just that most of us don't know it or think about it in those terms. He said just imagine what could be achieved if you were provided the knowledge and opportunity.

Bailey Cornog

During my time at Wayfair, I had the pleasure of working with Joe and his team. As a category manager at a major retailer, I've encountered a wide range of salespeople, ranging from the transactional folks who are just there to make a sale (which has always been ironic to me given Wayfair doesn't buy any inventory) to the 'relationship-oriented partners' (i.e. Joe).

From day one, I knew I could rely on Joe and his team to work with me to grow our mutual businesses. It's incredibly refreshing to work with a team that asks questions rather than coming with all the answers, a team that is receptive to fresh ideas and opportunities, a team that is reliable and follows through on promises, a team that is transparent and honest regarding roadblocks we inevitably faced yet committed to working closely to overcome challenges in a mutually beneficial manner.

Joe and his team bring a level of professionalism, respect and fun with them that is authentic and unparalleled. As a united team, we were able to achieve great business results, while also having a bit of fun. I'm grateful for the opportunity to work with and learn from Joe.

Preface

We are all 'buyers'. We buy things every day of our lives. We are all experts in buying, we just may not realise it. The reason we buy things is that we have a problem to solve. If you just moved into an apartment and you have nowhere to sleep, then you visit the bed store and buy a new bed. Your problem is solved. Nobody buys anything that does not solve a problem in their lives.

Every material thing in our daily lives must be bought. It follows that someone must sell those things.

If you look around the room you are sitting in you will be able to identify hundreds, if not thousands of items that have been sold, and in many cases those things have been sold 4 or 5 times before they reached your room. A small metal component that makes up part of your desk has been manufactured, sold to a wholesaler in bulk, perhaps exported to a distributor and then sold to the desk manufacturer, who has then sold it to you as part of your desk.

With each step in that supply chain a salesperson has negotiated with a buyer. A price agreement has been made and a sales commission earned. Has the salesperson 'sold' the item, or did the buyer simply 'buy' the item?

Salespeople must understand their role in this process. They must allow people to buy the best solution which solves their problem. If you start your sales career with this perspective, you will succeed.

Over the course of a long career in sales, Joe has developed a method of stepping a customer through the sales process and allowing them to buy exactly what they need. Joe has put his sales methodology into a book that is easy to read and should be a handbook for anyone starting out in a sales career.

Of course, the world has changed over the last 40 years. 'Old school' sales techniques may seem rather old fashioned with the advent of online marketplaces and social media marketing programs which can reach millions with the touch of a button. The fact is however, that the old school rules of engagement and the 'Denham Method' need to underpin your function within a business as a salesperson whether you are dealing face to face with a customer or with a faceless portal to a marketplace.

This book offers Joe's methodology, giving the young salesperson the basis of an attitude and process with which they should be working. The latter part of the book then applies this methodology to new marketplace retail platforms and gives the salesperson a strategy to deliver sales in a professional manner.

It is still the case that 'people buy from people'. If you are professional and work with the Denham Method, then people are more likely to buy from you.

Introduction

How do I go about being a salesman?

Do I need the gift of the gab? Do I have to be slick? Do I have to drive a 'rep's car' and do loads of mileage? Do I have to lie? Do I have to mislead the buyer? Do I have to 'con' the customers into buying my products?

The answer to all these questions is an emphatic 'no'!

This book lets you know the attributes you do need to build a professional and profitable career in sales. It is based on a system that I have devised over 40+ years of selling with very little formal training. I must emphasise that it is not product-specific training and can be applied to selling tins of beans or jet aircraft. For ease of reference, I will call the system 'The Denham Method' within the following pages.

During my career, I have sold specialist data communications equipment, telecoms equipment, specialist electrical fittings into the oil industry, medical products, electrical components, corporate promotional materials, furniture, beds, computer-based training contracts, garden products and a host of other things.

I have sold retail, door to door, through distribution networks, through agents, and I have also had my own TV show on Ideal World — a Sky Shopping Channel. I have sold directly to consumers (B2C) and business to business (B2B). At one point, in my last business, I had more than 400 sea containers 'on the water' being delivered to customers.

In all these products and sales channels, I have used the same system and methodology — either selling myself, or with a team of salespeople working with me (not under me), trained by me to use the same system. Most of my sales were made up of a lot of small value deals and some larger. When I was selling furniture, my average sale value was around $750. The biggest single sale I ever made was $13.5 million in 1997 — a computer training contract. The same methodology was used for each of these sales — this book demonstrates a technique that is applicable at all levels.

Once learned and applied, the Denham Method can be easily taught and used within a team environment. The advantage of this is that as salespeople come and go, perhaps take a holiday or are on sick leave, it is possible for another salesperson from your company to pick up where you left off with the customer very easily. Everyone in the team will be talking the same language regarding understanding what stage you are at within the sales cycle. If you do not understand the term 'sales cycle' don't worry, that's covered in chapters 3 and 4.

I have trained many salespeople. I have seen people perform well and others badly. Usually, the problem of poor performance is down to prematurely trying to close a deal before the sales cycle is complete, a lack of effort, or attempts to shortcut the way to success.

You can avoid the first two issues very easily. They are really training issues. If you read and follow the Denham Method within these pages, then you will not encounter these problems. The third is much more difficult to deal with. It usually applies to a young, ambitious person who is impatient to earn the big bucks. They generally do not realise that you cannot buy time or experience and feel that they are not progressing fast enough for the effort that they are putting in. This means that when they are offered a better starting salary with a rival, they jump at the opportunity.

They usually get the job because they interview well and are extremely ambitious; plus, they have been well trained by you! They start their new sales job and quickly realise they must start building their sales again with the new company and are back at the beginning. Decide what you want to sell and what industry interests you; then commit to it. Understand that it can take weeks or months and sometimes even years to build a profitable client base. There are no shortcuts to building your sales career.

This book is suitable for salespeople who are in a sales career and do not work to a methodology. They will usually find that they have lost sales and do not know why. They are usually very busy people with too much to do and too little time to do it. They sometimes forget to call customers and follow up on leads, often asking themselves, 'What happened to so and so who wanted XYZ product?' This book will teach you to utilise your current sales skills within a structured sales methodology and give you more time to actually sell to customers and therefore make more money.

The Denham Method is also suitable for sales managers who want to train new salespeople and manage salespeople who currently work for them. These are sales managers who do not know how many customers each of their sales staff are targeting, what specific markets they are aiming at, where their salespeople are within a given sales cycle and, most importantly, how much of the forecast sales revenue this month is real! This book will enable you to ensure a forecast revenue as far as is humanly possible. If you train and practise the Denham Method within your organisation, you will see immediate and significant results in terms of the increase in sales and reduction in your blood pressure!

Last and by no means least, this book is aimed at those people who want to get into a career in sales and do not know how to go about it. The book is really written for you. This could be a person who wants to run their own business but has no experience of sales. This book will teach you how to do it. Follow the Denham Method of sales and you will be far more professional, self-motivated, and successful than 98% of all those people out there who call themselves salespeople. You will succeed!

To end this introduction, I would like to tell you how I became a salesman. I left school at 18 and went to work for Barclays Bank. I quickly realised that my ambitions exceeded Barclays' pay structure and the sort of money I wanted to earn was going to take me 30 years to reach in a bank career that really didn't excite me anyway. I started looking at the job ads in a national newspaper (as you did, back then) and made an appointment with an employment agent in the City of London. This was the early 1980's and the stock market boom was happening. I was 19 years old and wanted a job as a stockbroker trainee or money dealer in the City.

The employment agent was in his early 50s with white hair and a look that said he had seen many ambitious 19-year-olds come and go through his well-trodden office doorway. Nevertheless, he was polite and courteous in his blue double-breasted blazer. I imagined him to be ex-military — he had that air about him.

As the interview went on it became apparent that I was too young and had too little experience to be taken on by one of the City banks and he asked me what I really wanted. I told him that I wanted the chance to get into something that made me want to get up in the morning and the chance to earn some real money. He then asked me if I had ever considered a career in sales. Now my view of the salesperson (like that of many people) was the stereotypical slick salesmen who had the gift of the gab, and I half took offence at his thinking that I had that ability. I answered as politely as I could that, no, I didn't want a career in sales.

As I was answering, he was flicking through a rolodex of cards on his desk, and he pulled a card out with a flourish.

'I have a job opportunity here. It is to demonstrate and sell Lear Jets. You get your own private jet assigned to you with a crew on standby 24 hours a day, 7 days a week; you then fly around the world picking up potential customers, demonstrating the jet and taking them to dinner with all expenses paid. The salary is a basic of $50,000 per annum and for every sale you get 1% of the sale value as commission with each jet normally selling for $50m. Lear salesmen normally sell 5 aircraft per year and your expected earnings are therefore around $2.5m per annum. Would you be interested?'

I took a naïve deep breath and managed to gasp, 'Yes, I'd be interested in that job.'

'Well son, there's selling and there's selling.' He put the card back in the rolodex and said, 'You must start somewhere, lad. It doesn't matter if you sell tins of beans or Lear jets, you cannot buy the experience and skills you need to get that job. You must go out there and gain it yourself.'

I left Barclays Bank the following month and got a job in a small data communications company as a salesman. The company was called Paxdata in Hemel Hempstead and the owner who gave me my start in sales was a man called Jim Fitzpatrick. I had set out on the road to gain the experience I needed to get that job selling Lear jets.

My new job involved selling modems to banks and commercial organisations. At the time, they were the only organisations who needed to send data around the world. Nobody really knew what a modem was. A year later the internet was invented. You can safely say, I was in the right place at the right time. Suddenly everyone needed a modem!

I started the new job and what happened next was interesting. I was given some comprehensive product training, a brief on the demographic of their typical customer and handed the keys to a company car. I attended a couple of customer calls with the other salesperson employed by the company and was then unleashed on the world in my new sales career.

Having worked at Barclays Bank dealing with many businesses, I was used to analysing business processes. But there seemed to be no business process applied to sales. You were simply expected to get out there and talk to customers hoping to uncover some business along the way.

As I learned my trade over the following two years, I developed a process to work with. I then followed that process throughout my career and taught it to every salesperson I worked with in my own businesses. The Denham Method is outlined in the following pages, and I am sure it will give you the success that your hard work deserves.

Some people view sales as an art. It's not an art, it is a business process like any other. If you apply the process, you will be a success.

1

What Does a Salesperson Do?

Before you read any further, close your eyes now and ask yourself 'What does a salesperson actually do? What is their core goal'?

What did you come up with? Ask this question to a classroom full of existing salespeople or trainees and you will normally get a mixture of the following answers:

- They demonstrate a company's products.
- They sell things.
- They get new customers for a company.
- They represent their company.
- They take orders from customers.

These things are not the 'core goal'. They may perform some of the functions mentioned above, however, what a salesperson really does is 'generate cash'.

Here ends the first lesson. Your job as a salesperson is to generate cash for the business you work for. Your job has not been completed until the customer's money is in your company's bank account.

This is the job any company will employ you for even if you dropped out of high school without even a swimming certificate. If you have the ability and a demonstrable track record in generating cash for a company, I can absolutely guarantee that a managing director will give you a sales job within his organisation.

If you go about your job with that in the forefront of your mind — 'my job is to generate cash' — you will be thinking in the correct way that will lead you to success.

There are different kinds of sales jobs and the Denham Method is used in all of them. For example, you could be employed by a company as a sole salesperson for that company. You could be employed within a company as part of a team, but with your own given territory (either geographical or market territory), or you could be employed by yourself selling a product that you have bought or even invented and put into production.

Whatever your situation, I am going to ask you to regard your sales position in the same way. You should think of yourself as a profit centre. If you are employed, you should understand what your cost is to the company. Your basic salary, your car, your expenses as well as hidden costs (health care, pensions for example) should be included. You should also be aware that the company will be making a large investment in you up front before you produce any sales to start paying them back.

You are a one-person profit centre, and you should be very aware of the fact that you are a loss to the company if you have cost the company more than the profit you have generated in your sales or a profitable asset to the company if you have made more profit from the margin in your sales than you have cost the company.

You cannot do your job properly if you do not understand the company that you work for and how much profit and cost are involved with their product or service. Let me give you an example:

Example One: Ace Low Tech Toy Distribution

Ace is a one-man band organisation. It buys a yo-yo from China in bulk. It buys them for $1 each and sells them on a market stall in the local town centre for $2 each. The cost of the stall is $50 rent and the travel cost to get there and back each week is $5.

The company's weekly cost is therefore $55. It therefore needs to sell 55 yo-yo's (at $1 profit) each week to break even. Every yo-yo thereafter puts $1 profit into the salesperson's pocket. If they sell 100 yo-yos this week, they have made $45 profit.

Easy, isn't it?

Example Two: Ace High Tech Company Ltd

This company manufactures and sells a range of electronic testing equipment and sells through distributors who, in turn sell to shops, who in turn sell to 'end users'. Their main product is the 'Ace Live Tester Tool'. The tool sells in the shops for $99. The shop needs a margin of 25%. Therefore, the distributor sells it to the shop for $75. The distributor also needs 25%. He therefore buys the product for $50. If you represent the manufacturer and sell to the distributor you can therefore expect your sales value to be $50 for the tool.

The company also sells the tool through another channel — a direct sales website. In this instance the tool is discounted to the end user and sells for $89. The website needs to earn 20% and you therefore sell to the website at $71.

The physical cost of the manufacturing of the tool is $25 (components and parts which the company buys). The company then has costs of rent, manufacturing staff, and a research and development staff to come up with new and exciting products for the market. It also has sales (your cost) and marketing costs to account for.

In this example you should know that your 'gross profit margin' on the Ace Live Tester Tool' is $25 (when sold through distribution) and $46 (when sold through the website). However, you will not know what the other company costs are and therefore what the company's break-even point is, i.e., how many tools they need to sell every month before all costs are covered and they make a profit.

The reality is that the all the costs mentioned above are usually spread over many products, each one with different gross profit margins and usually to a mixture of distribution or direct sales — therefore different margins.

Even if the managing director of the company knows the answer, which they usually don't, you will never know how many you must sell to make the company profitable. It depends how many you sell through distribution or online in any given month and a host of other factors.

Not so easy, is it?

It is therefore imperative that you work as an individual profit centre within this company. You need to know the gross profit margin on the product or products that you are selling and agree sales targets with your manager that ensure the company is happy with your performance and that you are comfortable that you are profitable and therefore a success. Use of the Denham Method will teach you to do this.

2

How Much Do You Want to Earn?

Do not take a sales position that does not pay an agreed commission (percentage of sale value) based on your sales performance. There is no incentive to improve your sales or work towards the growth of your company if you are not paid a commission.

Usually, sales salaries are made up of a 'basic' salary and an 'OTE' or On Target Earnings figure. An example would be:

Basic Salary	$12,000 pa [per annum]
OTE	$50,000 pa

This represents a sales commission of 5% of sales value with an agreed annual sales target of $760,000.

In other words, the company will pay you $1,000 per month to turn up for work (your basic salary). If you sell $760,000 worth of their products in a year, they will pay you 5% of that in commission ($38,000) giving you total earnings of $50,000 pa (your OTE).

There are many slight permutations to this formula depending on the company and structure. For example, they may pay the commission as a percentage of profit margin rather than sales value. They may insist that you achieve a minimum value in sales before they begin to pay commission monthly. In the above example, the monthly target is $63,333 in sales. They may insist that you achieve a minimum of $50,000 before they pay any commission at all in any given month.

Some short-sighted companies also insist on a 'cap' on earnings for their salespeople. I suggest that you do not take any sales position where there is a cap on commission earnings.

If I am a managing director and one of my salespeople (as has been the case) has had such a good month that they have earned more in commission than my salary, I have never once objected to paying them. They earned their good fortune, took the risk of the job, and almost certainly many months when they weren't earning their OTE.

You must understand how you are being paid and work towards maximising yourself as a profit centre and therefore your earnings.

So how much do you want to earn? Well, look at your salary package and work it out! I like to do this back to front. I do not care about my OTE figure (unless I am paid a bonus when I reach it)!

'I want to earn $100,000 this year'. Simple enough statement to make. Now how do I go about it?

I am paid a basic of $12,000; therefore, I need to earn $88,000 in commission. My commission rate is 5% of sales value; therefore, I need to sell $1,760,000 of product this year to earn my $88,000 commission. My product sells for $99 each. Therefore, I need to sell 17,778 of them. I can then break this down to 1,482 per month.

That's my personal target set — better get on with it!

In summary:

- Review your salary package and understand how it works.
- Work out how much you want to earn.
- Set your own personal target.
- Break it down so you know how much you need to sell every month.

3

A Structured Approach: The Sales Cycle

Most people who work in sales understand what a 'sales cycle' is. If you are one of those people bear with me, there is more to it than you may know.

The 'sales cycle' is the term used to describe the steps that are taken when proceeding through a sale with a customer. An example would be:

1. Initial contact with a customer.
2. Identify Requirements.
3. Offer/prove solution.
4. Offer quotation.
5. Take order.
6. Deliver solution.
7. Get paid.

The sales cycle is usually expressed in time and, with experience, can be worked out so that you have an idea of how long the sales cycle is for your product. A sales cycle can be minutes, days, weeks, months or even years, depending upon the product. A good example would be a company selling tractors. The sales cycle could go as follows:

1. INITIAL CONTACT — The salesperson may meet a local farmer at a county show in June. This is an initial introduction. He shows the farmer around the product range and offers to visit the farm. As it is a busy time of year, the farmer suggests autumn as a good time.
2. IDENTIFY REQUIREMENTS — The salesperson calls the farmer in October and makes an appointment to

visit later that month. During the visit he asks questions to ascertain if the farmer has any immediate or future requirements. The farmer mentions that he has plans to start a new product range and will need a tractor that is more powerful and can pull more weight than his current model. In starting the new product range, it is essential that he has reliable equipment as they will be understaffed in the first year and will not be able to afford breakdowns. The salesperson takes details of the specific needs of the farmer and offers to go back to the office, talk to several manufacturers and find the right solution. During the visit, the farmer mentions that planting of the new product will be done in April, although he will only need the more powerful tractor in August when he needs to harvest the crop.

3. OFFER SOLUTION — After talking to the various manufacturers, the salesperson identifies two possible alternative solutions for the farmer. He draws up a detailed quotation (solution A and solution B) with the various brochures and technical information and presents them to the farmer by appointment in November. The salesman also talks to a couple of his customers who currently own both types of tractor and asks them if they would be willing to allow him to visit with the new customer and talk to them about their effectiveness. The potential new customer thinks this a great idea and that they could meet in the New Year.

4. PROVE SOLUTION — Again, by appointment, the salesperson collects the farmer and visits his existing customers to see the tractors working. It is now February. The customer likes what he sees and enjoys the visit with likeminded people. In the end and after seeing both solutions, he decides that solution B is

best for him although he wants a slightly changed specification to meet with the budget figure he had in mind. The salesperson goes back to the office and re-draws the proposal to the customer.

5. TAKE ORDER — He presents this proposal early in March to the customer and invites him to lunch to meet his Service Manager. During the lunch, the customer is made to feel very confident about the level of after sales service he will receive from the company once he places an order with them. The Service Manager is a most pleasant person who shows his technical knowledge of the equipment and an understanding of the farmer's daily problems and time constraints. He goes on to explain that they have a guaranteed 4-hour call out during the working summer months for any breakdowns. The salesperson and farmer shake hands on the deal and the farmer says he will place an order. The salesperson visits the farm with his order book later that month and completes a signed order for a new tractor based on his revised proposal. The tractor is on a 3-month delivery schedule from the factory.

6. DELIVER SOLUTION — The tractor arrives from the factory and is delivered to the farmer at the beginning of July.

7. GET PAID — The farmer is invoiced and makes payment at the beginning of August. This is the exact time of year that the farmer needed the tractor to cut and process his new crop.

This has been a sales cycle of 14 months to sell a tractor, and I would suggest that, for this particular industry, this is about average. There are products that have much faster sales cycles. For example, a salesperson selling dish cloths door to door has a sales cycle of less than a minute!

You need to apply this logic to your product in your industry and your marketplace; you will ascertain a rough idea of the average sales cycle for your product. It is important that you know and understand the length of time it takes to sell your product as this will determine your forecasting accuracy and ability as well as your own expectation of earnings.

For all you existing salespeople reading this, you will have come this far in the chapter and be thinking, 'Well, tell me something that I don't know.' What I have described so far is fairly common knowledge and methodology for any salesperson. Well, here's the bit I asked you to bear with me for — did you know that every customer also has a buying cycle?

One of the most common faults of any salesperson and a main reason for failure in completing the sale is that they do not understand this simple fact. They go blindly through the 'sales cycle', ticking off the bits they think they have completed and fail to understand that the customer may not be fully through their 'buying cycle'. What is worse, most customers do not even consciously know that they are going through a buying cycle! Let me explain.

1. I am hungry.
2. What do I fancy? Let me see. Some chocolate. That would hit the spot.
3. I visit the store and am confronted with at least 50 chocolate bars to choose from. I like Twix and I like Mars Bars.
4. I have a look at how much change is in my pocket. I have 70 cents. The Mars Bar is 80 cents and the Twix is 68 cents.
5. I buy the Twix and eat it. That hit the spot!

What I have just been through is a 'buying cycle' and everybody does this every time they buy something. The order of events goes:

1. I have a problem (I'm hungry).
2. I need to find a solution (visit the store and see what they have).
3. Prove the solution (what would best stop my hunger—a Mars or a Twix).
4. Budget (how much money do I have for this).
5. Buy it and solve the problem (buy the Twix within budget and eat it).

Everybody does this every time they buy something—even if they do not know they are doing it. A professional buyer working for a large corporation may understand this process (in my experience, many do not). However, most times a customer will not consciously understand that this is a definitive process they are going through. Here comes the clever bit. Let's put them together.

When we put the sales cycle and buying cycle alongside each other, it looks like this:

Sales Cycle	Buying Cycle
Initial contact with a customer	I have a problem
Identify Requirements	Find a possible solution
Offer/prove solution	Prove the solution
Offer quotation	Budget
Take order	Buy
Deliver solution	My problem is solved
Get paid	Pay

You will notice that when put alongside each other, the sales and buying cycles tie in very nicely. If you as a salesperson understand that you are guiding your customer through a buying cycle (which they may not be aware of), you will get the deal 9 times out of 10.

The problem often comes when the salesperson gets to the end of their sales cycle and asks for an order. The customer is not forthcoming and avoids contact or puts you off for some reason. You do not get the deal and you cannot understand why. The reason is simple — you may have completed your sales cycle, but the customer has not completed their buying cycle. It could be the most insignificant detail (in the salesperson's mind) that means that the customer is not happy that the solution you have offered will solve their problem.

In the farm example for instance, the salesperson took note that the farmer had mentioned that he would not be able to afford breakdowns in starting his new product range as he would be understaffed. He therefore made sure that he introduced the farmer to his Service Manager in such a way (over lunch) that a trust relationship could be formed, and the farmer left that meeting feeling that the service and after sales care for his new investment was sound. If he had not done this, there may have been an element of doubt in the farmer's mind about the backup service and therefore he may have looked elsewhere for a solution. In other words, the solution the salesperson offered would not have been proved in the customer's mind. In this case, the salesperson would arrive at the end of the sales cycle, ask for the order, and not receive it. In this instance, they almost certainly would never know why.

In understanding the buying and sales cycles you will be in control of the sales process. In summary you must:

- Identify the sales cycle for your product.
- Identify your customers' buying cycle (they are all different).
- Never try to shortcut the process.

How do you do this? Mainly by asking the right questions— more in the next chapter!

I said earlier that 'every buying cycle starts with a problem'. But what if you sell garden furniture sets to garden centres on a wholesale basis, what possible 'problem' could the customer have that they want you to solve? Well, they have the problem that they must make the maximum profit possible with limited floor space, whilst offering their customers a range of reasonably priced products. Your sale becomes less about the product and more about how your customer can maximise their revenue utilising your product and marketing backup. Their buying process again starts with them having a problem — lack of profit. You can solve that for them by providing the right product that sells!

4

Moving through the Sales Cycle

Now that you understand there is a sales cycle *and* a buying cycle, how do we get to the end of it and get the deal? The answer is surprisingly simple. You 'step' through the sales process and 'guide' your customer through their buying process (remember that they may not consciously know they are going through a buying cycle). The only way you will do this is in complete communication with your customer and by asking 'open' questions that enable you to foresee any problems in the sale.

I mentioned at the end of the last chapter that every customer's buying cycle is different, and this is true. You must ask questions of the customer to get an understanding of their buying process. For example, a large corporation may have to get the budget approved and signed off by the Chief Accountant. If you as a salesperson didn't realise this and blindly went through the sales cycle, you may have reached the end only to discover that you did not get the deal because the Chief Accountant did not leave enough money in the budget for your deal. Your customer would be forced to accept a cheaper quotation from a competitor that they did not actually want! If you knew about the company process and made an early presentation to the Chief Accountant; showing them the advantages that your more expensive solution would bring, they may well have allowed more money in the budget for the project.

Ask 'open' questions. If? What? When? Why? How? These are all words that require more than yes or no answers. In this way you will gain information from the customer that will enable you to understand their buying process and help you fit the correct solution to their problem.

Here's the sales and buying cycle again:

Sales Cycle	Buying Cycle
Initial contact with a customer	I have a problem
Identify Requirements	Find a possible solution
Offer / prove solution	Prove the solution
Offer quotation	Budget
Take order	Buy
Deliver solution	My problem is solved
Get paid	Pay

Once you have identified both your sales cycle and your customer's buying cycle, it is possible to break them down into a series of 'little sales'. After each step has been completed (in both columns) you must qualify and 'close' the step with the customer and proceed to the next step. In other words, ask the customer if they are happy with what has been discussed and agreed so far and therefore happy to proceed to the next step.

When I was working a sales territory, I wanted to maximise my income. I would therefore go as far as asking the customer, 'Are you happy with what we have agreed so far? I do not want to go ahead and waste your time or mine in tying up both our resources if you are not ready.' If he or she answered yes, then that 'little sale' was closed, and we could move on to the next step in the sales/buying process. If they answered no, then I made a later appointment when they said they would be ready.

So, if you qualify and close the 'little sales' at each step and confirm that the customer is happy, you will arrive at the end of your sales cycle and (to the best of your knowledge) the end of the customer's buying cycle. Then what? Simply ask for the order!

I have never believed in clever 'closing techniques'. The fact of the matter is that if you have done your job correctly to this point, there is no need to be clever—you have qualified and closed at each step—just ask for the order.

If you are embarrassed and have trouble doing this, the best method is simply to hold out your hand to the customer (as if to shake) and ask, 'Can I have your business?' If you are right and your customer has been qualified and 'closed' at each step in the process, they will shake your hand and say yes! Your first deal—congratulations!

What if they say no?

Then you have misjudged the completion of their steps through their buying process and simply need to re-address each step to find out where the problem is. Put simply, if the customer has an objection to placing an order you need to overcome it. The first thing to do is find out what the objection is and if it is 'real'. The best way to do this is with the 'if/would' line of questioning. You'll see what I mean.

'Can I have the order please?'

'Not at the moment.'

'Why? What's the problem?'

'Well, I need a couple of days to think about it before we place the order.'

'So, if I make an appointment to see you in say, 3 days, would you place the order?'

At this point they will say yes or no! If they say yes, then you have closed and have the order at the next appointment; if they say no, then this shows that the initial objection is not real and there is something else that is stopping the order. At this point you again ask 'why?'

'Why?'

'Well actually, I am a bit concerned about the power rating of your product. I have not seen it working and I am not sure that it will meet our needs.'

'So, if I can show you that the product demonstrates the correct power rating, would you place the order?'

Again, at this point, the customer will say yes or no. If they say yes, then arrange a demonstration to 'prove' the power rating of the product and you have the deal. If they say no, then again, you must ask 'why' and use the 'if/would' questions to find the real objection and solve it. Eventually, you will get to the real reason that the customer is wavering and solve the problem. Remember, simply go back to each step of the sales/ buying cycle; requalify and ask for the order again.

Never be afraid to ask if/would questions several times. You are just doing your job.

What if their initial objection is real and justified? You must remember that your customer has a problem to solve. Your solution must genuinely solve their problem. If it does not, then you cannot reasonably expect to get the sale. However, you can turn real objections around to your advantage.

Let me give you an example. In selling the tractor to our farmer customer, we come to the end of the sales cycle and ask for the order. He says no, claiming it is more expensive than the competitor's equivalent offering. There is no getting around it, this is a real objection! The first thing you must do is agree with the customer (in part). Many salespeople fall into the trap at this point of starting an argument with the customer, along the lines of—'well if you want a cheaper product, I think that's a foolish move'. What you have done is called the customer a fool and you have more chance of getting milk out of his pig than getting an order from him after that.

You should therefore agree (in part) to his real objection to show that you understand it. Something along the lines of—'I understand that price is a major concern to any farmer in an industry where margins are so tight'. This shows the farmer that you respect his opinion and understand his objection.

You can then turn this around to your advantage. You have genuine respect for him and his opinion. He will therefore listen to genuine reason and make his decision accordingly. Something along the lines of, 'However, could I ask you to think about the long-term cost implications of going with our competitor?

You are aware that we have a guaranteed 4 hour call out on breakdowns and the extra $1,000 you spend with us now could save you many thousands in "down time" over the next 5 years. Our warranty is also 12 months longer than the competitors and this alone is worth the extra investment in the long run.'

At this point the customer will make a considered buying judgement. Are the extra services that you offer worth more than the $1,000 that you are charging for them? If they are not worth the extra money to him and you have no margin left to play with in discount, then shake hands and part as friends. He will give you another chance next time he needs a problem solved. However, I bet he gives you the deal!

The point is this. We do not actually sell anything as 'salespeople'. What we do is show people our solutions and allow them to buy from us. If a person has a problem (and all sales start because a customer has a problem), then they must find a solution. Your job is simply to show them your solution to the best of your ability in a professional manner. If what you offer is a 'value for money' solution to the problem, they will buy it.

Often the most difficult element of the sales cycle is the proving stage. Your customer must be confident that the product they are buying will solve their problem. This is often where the salesperson loses the sale and often does not understand why that has happened. For example, a customer may ask to 'test' or 'evaluate' a product before they buy. You leave a test sample of the product with the customer and then call them a week later to see if the customer is happy to proceed. Most times you will get an answer something like, 'Oh it's still under my desk. I haven't had a chance to look at it yet'; or 'Oh we had a quick look, and we don't think it will be suitable.' You have lost the sale and you do not know why.

In this scenario it is imperative that you retain control. If a customer asks to test the product, ask them what they want to test! Are they testing the function of the product? The durability? Are they testing to see if the colour matches their décor? Are they going to show the product to anyone else in the company to get their approval? Establish the parameters of the testing and put a success criterion in place. 'So, if the product performs x function and the MD likes it, can we agree to proceed?'

If the customer answers yes, then rather than leaving a test sample on an open-ended basis, suggest a meeting with them and the Managing Director, go in (with a technical assistant if necessary), and demonstrate the product.

Alternatively, leave the product with the buyer after agreeing the success criterion and then make an appointment for 2 days' time to collect the sample and confirm that it met their needs.

What you are doing is retaining control of the sale. We always set a date to move forward through the sales cycle and we agree a success criterion that gets us there.

In summary:

- Ask 'open' questions.
- Get positive answers.
- Guide your customer through each step of the sales cycle ensuring that they are also stepping through their buying cycle.
- Close each step as you go and confirm this with the customer.
- Find the customer's real objection and overcome it.
- For customer evaluations, set a success criterion.
- Retain control.

5

The Sales Pipeline

What do we mean by the sales 'pipeline'? Well, the pipeline is simply the number of customers we have introduced into an active 'sales cycle'. I like to view it as a funnel. Something like this:

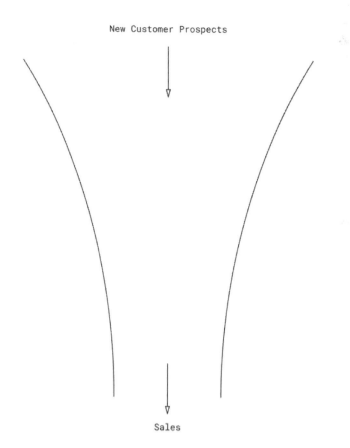

We introduce potential new customers into the pipeline (the top of the funnel) and what comes out of the bottom is sales.

As the prospective customers move through the pipeline and the various stages of the cycle, we will lose some along the way. Perhaps our solution was not right for them. Perhaps our solution was too expensive. Perhaps they solved their problem another way. This is natural.

We can expect a win ratio of around 20% in the early days. As you become better at customer targeting and qualifying if your solution is right for that customer earlier, then this win ration will improve.

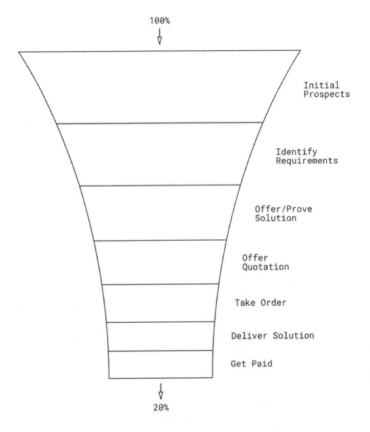

The 20% ratio figure can be applied in several ways. You can work it on the number of customers you speak to or the value of the sales revenue they represent. Applying this ratio, if you want to get $100K in sales then you need to introduce prospective customers with deals worth $500K into the pipeline.

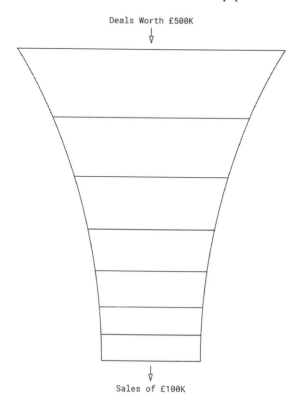

Deals Worth £500K

Sales of £100K

You already know what your average sales value is. Let's say it is $10K per sale. Therefore, you need 10 sales to make your $100K target that month. You can plainly see that you need to be speaking to 50 new prospective customers to achieve your goal.

As a professional salesperson you should very regularly go through the exercise of working out how many customers you need in pipeline to meet your target. You should do this with an eye on how much money you want to earn and therefore you will know how hard you have must work to achieve it. It will also prompt you to block book a day to call new customers and introduce them to the pipeline on a regular basis. It rapidly becomes obvious when you fail to do this and starve the pipeline leading to a slump in sales in the not-too-distant future.

Feeding new customers into the pipeline is imperative to your ongoing success. It tends to be the first thing that gets left behind as you become busier meeting the needs of current sales prospects. Do not let this happen. Make time to feed the pipeline regularly with new prospects.

In summary:

- Look at the customer deals in a visual way so you can easily see where they are in pipeline.
- Expect to close 20% of the deals you introduce into pipeline.
- Make time to keep introducing new customers no matter how busy you are.

6

Secret Tools of a Salesperson

Some are obvious and not so 'secret', others you may not have thought about. This chapter is about giving you a few tips on how to make the best impression and get the result you want — win the order!

Body Language

As a salesperson you are in a constant information gathering and negotiating role. As such, you need to ensure that your body language does not betray your thoughts. As an example, it may be that you dislike the person you are selling to. That is of no real importance. You should still be professional in your conduct and approach. However, be aware that your body language can give you away.

In simple terms, ensure that you portray an 'open' demeanour and that your body language shows that you are honest and understanding. 'Closed' and 'tight' body language suggests that you have something to hide or are being dishonest. Next time you buy something from a 'salesperson' notice their body language. You will be amazed at your perception of them and what they are saying simply from how they conduct themselves without speaking!

There are hundreds of books about body language. Learn all you can about the subject. It will help you win more business.

Physical Presence and Presentation

It should go without saying that your physical presentation and appearance should be beyond criticism. Dirty or unkempt hair, nails, clothes and shoes will lose you 9 deals out of 10 even if you have the best product in the world. People buy from people and your appearance goes a long way to getting over the initial introduction stage.

Your dress should be appropriate for your industry and your marketplace. Selling IT equipment in the City of London will mean that you dress in a business suit. Selling a tractor to a farmer means that you should dress smartly with a collared shirt and with appropriate clothing for visiting a farm. You should still be clean and presentable.

There is no excuse for losing a deal because of your appearance. Wear appropriate clothing or take the chance of severely reducing your earnings capacity. This is not being old fashioned; it is being realistic. I know because I am one of your potential customers.

Environment

Meet your customers in an appropriate environment where you can talk without interruption and where it is conducive to getting business done. If they sit within a very busy office with people coming to and fro constantly, diplomatically suggest that you meet outside their office, perhaps at the coffee shop across the street. You will often find that they are glad to get out of their environment for a while and you can guarantee their attention.

A word of caution. If you decide to meet customers in a restaurant, pub or bar, be aware of how much they and you are drinking. Be aware of the impression you are giving. Customer entertainment and a couple of beers on expenses (if you are not driving) can be very positive in building the relationship. Getting blasted and making a fool of yourself, or worse, your customer making a fool of themselves, is quite another. You have been warned.

Asking Loaded Questions

Asking 'loaded' questions is an effective way to achieve a positive outcome from any conversation. Think about your product, industry and customer's problems and ask questions that will give answers which automatically enable you to steer the conversation in a positive light towards your product. This gets easier with practise and some thought beforehand.

A car salesperson could ask a customer, 'What features would you like to see on your new car?' And hope that he will list some of those that she has to offer with her product. Alternatively, she could ask a 'loaded' question such as, 'Have you ever been caught in a traffic jam on the highway on a boiling hot day? Isn't it hell?' On hearing the customer response, she may then like to mention that air conditioning is included at no extra cost on the model she is proposing to the customer. Loaded questions are a very positive weapon in the salesperson's armoury.

Getting Positive Answers

Somewhat allied to asking loaded questions is the desire to get positive answers from your customer. Again, this takes practise, but soon you will notice immediately when you have asked a 'wrong' question and get a negative answer from your customer.

The reason positive answers are important is very simple. It gets the customer in a positive frame of mind and more likely to be positive when you ask for the order. It really is as simple as that. If you ask a customer a series of questions, all of which the answer to is positive in some way, then when you ask for the order, he is infinitely more likely to be positive again. Try it, it works!

Use of Prior Knowledge

If you have knowledge perhaps about a customer's business or market that the customer does not realise you know, this can be a very powerful tool in steering the customer positively to you and your product, but only if you use it in the right way. For example, before visiting a customer for the first time you look at their website and see an announcement that they are looking to move their head office and expand their operation. You are selling a new telephone system to the company. You might like to mention in your initial presentation to the customer that the telephone system you are offering is fully transportable and, in fact, your company offers a relocation and installation service at no extra cost in the first year after purchase. 'That's a coincidence,' says your customer, we are looking to move premises this year. I was going to put off the purchase, but if you would re-locate the system for us at no extra charge, there's no reason not to go ahead with you.' Coincidences are amazingly positive things in my experience.

Listen

Sounds silly eh? Listen. There, I said it again. It still sounds silly! You would be amazed at the number of salespeople I have met over the years who did not have the ability to listen. All they want to do is spout off about their amazing product and are not really interested in what the customer has to say. If you are a salesperson, you will read this and I guarantee, over the next few weeks will catch yourself talking a lot about your product and not listening to your customer. Your customer will buy. You just need to shut up for a minute, listen to their problem and steer them towards the correct solution that you have to offer.

What is the point in asking open questions (What? Why? How? Who? When?) when you are not prepared to shut up and listen to the answer? Don't be a salesperson who loves the sound of their own voice. You will not win orders that way.

Using Pauses (When to Shut Up)

You should learn when to wait for a little while before speaking. It is often the case that, when we have the perfect solution for a customer, we get excited as salespeople at the prospect of winning the order. It is very easy to gabble on and not allow the customer time to think through his buying decision and actually buy. When you ask for the order, shut up and wait for the customer to reply. If he does not respond immediately, stay quiet. Let her think about it, let her answer.

As a customer, whenever a salesperson visiting me asks me for an order, I do not answer them. I wait to see what they do when all they get back from me is silence. The canny ones shut up and wait for me to answer, even if the pause goes on for what seems like an embarrassingly long period of time. The less experienced salespeople, embarrassed by the silence, jump in and say something like, 'Or do you need a slightly better price?' Try it next time you buy something, you will be amazed how many salespeople cannot shut up. Don't be one of them.

Getting the Customer to Buy: Allowing Her to Sell to Herself

Sometimes you will come across a customer who very much knows her own mind and wants very little help in the buying process. In these cases, they will ask very pertinent questions and expect thoroughly honest, concise, and accurate replies to those questions. They will then tell you how and when they want to proceed. Take my advice; let them call the shots and, unless they are requesting anything unreasonable from you or your company, just allow them to sell to themselves. Again, you would be amazed at the number of salespeople who lose the deal because they insist on completing their 'sales cycle' without reference to the way the customer wants to do business.

I have a good example for you. Many years ago I needed some new clothes for my TV show on the Shopping Channel. I walked into a local shop. Before the door had closed behind me I was asked, 'Can I help you, Sir?' Not an unreasonable request. 'No thanks,' I replied, 'I would just like to look around.' 'Certainly Sir.'

I managed to get to the first rack of shirts before he was there again. 'We have that in blue as well.' I left. He wasn't listening.

In the next shop, the Manager greeted me as I entered and left me to look around. Within half an hour I had spent $2,000 picking things from the rack that I liked. When I had a query, I asked him and he answered, he then left me alone to shop in peace. He could see that I knew my own mind, knew what I was looking for, and that if allowed, I would sell to myself. He was right and found a good customer. That's a true story. Tony in The Squires Room on Colchester High Street — a great salesman!

Believe In Your Product and Yourself

If you do not believe that the product you are selling is the correct solution for your customer, get another product or find the right customer. If, however, you have the right solution, then you should believe it completely. Your belief in yourself, your company and your product will come shining through. Your customer will believe that she has made the right decision when she orders from you.

For this reason, I have never gone to work for a company or for myself without believing that the product I was selling has truly unique advantages in the marketplace and was the best solution available. Notice I did not say cheapest.

Maintain a Positive Attitude

When you have read this book fully you will realise that sales is a 'numbers game', and what that phrase actually means. For every customer order you win, there will be many that you do not. This can be for a variety of reasons, most of which you have no control over whatsoever. You will be told 'no' 99 times before you get a 'yes', and some days you will wish you hadn't bothered to get out of bed.

It is very important that you realise that you have to go through the 99 'nos' before you get the 'yes' you are looking for. Sales as a profession is difficult, demanding, hard work. It is important that you maintain a supremely positive attitude throughout. If you are on your 99th 'no' for the month and you go into that next meeting with a face like a wet weekend you will not get the deal! That 'yes' can come anytime, and you must give every customer, every presentation, every call your best shot. I can assure you, the 'yes' will come!

No Bullshit

Sorry to put it so bluntly, but there you are. There's no better way of putting it in my opinion. If you try to bullshit a customer, just once, you will be found out and you will lose the deal. If a customer asks a question that you do not know the answer to then say so. Make a note of it, find out the answer and come back to the customer afterwards. The customer will respect you so much more than you realise. It is also a great way to pin your customer down to a follow up meeting if you think about it!

If you know the answer, speak with confidence. If you do not, say so and go and find the answer. Do not guess. 'I wouldn't bullshit a customer,' I hear you say! Sometimes you can't help yourself — the temptation is too great. Don't do it.

Stick to Fact: Do Not Sell 'Smoke and Mirrors'

Do not spread rumour about an industry, market, product, or competitor. If you have heard within your company that an upgrade for one of your products is possibly coming, wait until it is fact before telling your customers. If you try to sell current or future products on anything less than fact, you will come undone in the sales process and the customer will never buy from you again.

Tell the Truth

It goes without saying really, doesn't it? But there will come a time, possibly through no fault of your own when there is a temptation to lie to a customer about a product or perhaps a delivery date, or something else to help get the sale. The profession you have chosen is sometimes pressurised and a lot, including your salary, rides on your success. Do not do it. Even if you get away with it the first time, eventually you will be caught out.

If you have the right product, the right solution, the right service, and a professional approach to your customers you do not need to lie. If something goes wrong — you made a mistake in a quotation or you got a specification wrong for example — Simply contact the customer, admit the mistake, tell her the truth and ask how she wants to proceed. Or, better still, offer a solution to solve the problem. Do not lie. It doesn't reflect well on you, your company or your profession.

Focus on Product Strengths

Or, do not dwell on your less positive features. This may seem obvious but again, I frequently see salespeople who insist on dwelling on the less positive features of their products, especially when they are selling against a strong competitor. Perhaps it is a sub-conscious thing when they realise that a competitor has a slightly better feature than they have, that they then must dwell on it.

The best example is in visiting an electrical retail store. Do a little research on the internet first and ask a salesperson to show you the latest television. He will go through it feature by feature. When he mentions a specific feature, ask him how it compares to a specific competitor (who you know has a better screen resolution for example). Notice that 9 times out of 10 an average salesperson will sub-consciously dwell on the screen resolution feature, stumble, and fumble through the rest of the presentation. He will dwell on the negative, thinking that you have 'found him out' and that he is not going to get the sale.

The brightest salespeople realise that they cannot 'out-feature' every competitor. The buying process is part of an overall decision-making process by the customer and having a slightly lower screen resolution (in this example) will not matter in the overall presentation, as long as you do not dwell on it, move forward and accentuate the positives that you have instead.

Remember: focus on the strengths of you, your company, and your product.

Never, Ever Badmouth the Competition

It will make you feel better but will lose you the sale.

Understand Her Personal Objectives

Customers and specifically buyers within corporations are motivated by different objectives. You need to understand this and find out what your buyer's objectives are.

Are they trying to find the best solution for their company? Are they trying to find the cheapest solution? Are they trying to spend their budget before year-end? If your buyer does well on this project, will she be promoted? What are her personal objectives?

Find out if there is a personal objective within the project or deal that you can help her with. If you help her in her objective, she is more likely to award the deal to you. As an example, when I was selling computer training contracts, our sales contact (buyer) was often based in the IT department of a large corporation. When your career is in this environment, it is essential that you keep pace with the latest innovations and developments in the IT world. This is not so easy when you have your head down in a programming project for 18 months at a time.

I would ask the buyer what specific courses she personally would like to take in the next 12 months. I would then make sure that, as part of my proposal, those specific courses were added to the ones they had asked for. In this way, my buyer could keep herself updated with the necessary skills she personally needed as well as get a great deal for her company. It usually meant that I got the deal as well!

I have already said people buy from people and when you can help a buyer with a personal objective without doing anything underhand, it will always help you to win the deal.

Bonus Points

Buyers in a corporate environment are often in competition with other buyers for promotion. If you can get an understanding of the buyer's situation within the company, you will often find that she has personal political objectives to achieve. This means that you can personally assist her. Bringing a project in on time, solving a very difficult budget dilemma, finding a solution to a problem that has dogged a long running project; anything that will earn the buyer 'bonus points' within her organisation will often help you to win the deal.

Light Her Candle

Every person is interested in different things. For example, when selling a car you may find that your buyer is more interested in the horsepower of the engine and how many cylinders it has. Another buyer may be more interested in the comfort level of the car. Yet another may be more interested in the fuel economy.

By asking 'open' questions you will discover what aspect most appeals to your buyer — which one 'lights her candle'. Once found, you may concentrate on this aspect of the car a little more than the others. In a sticky moment during the negotiation, it is a useful tool to be able to steer the conversation back to the aspect of your product that you know most delights the customer.

Keep Control: Direct the Meeting

Always remember that you are following a sales cycle and that your customer Is following her buying process. However, later in the book you will discover the importance of your time management and the need to maximise your 'sales time'. Buyers can be lonely creatures who like to talk about the pet project they have right now. Whilst it is important that you understand your customer's requirements, it is also important that you move the sale forward — closing the 'little sales' as you go and making sure that each step in the sales process is qualified and closed.

Keep control of the sale. Make sure that, at each step, you direct the sale forward to the next stage. Make an appointment to get the next thing done. Take action with your customer, creating dates and appointments to follow through. You should never find yourself in a situation within a sales cycle where you do not completely know what is supposed to happen next to make that sale come to fruition. Direct the way forward if your customer is not doing so.

7

Features and Benefits

I have met some very experienced salespeople who, when meeting a customer for the first time and are asked to present their product, simply go through a list of the features of their product hoping to find a feature that the customer likes. Customer presentations become boring and no more than an exercise in reading off the list of features that appears on the back of your product literature.

The best salespeople understand that customers do not buy 'features'. They buy the 'benefits' that those features give them. To explain this principle, let's look at a salesperson selling a new car. The features of the car are as follows:

Features

2 Litre Hybrid Powered
Segregated air conditioning
Alloy wheels
Rear seat entertainment system
Panoramic sunroof
Keyless entry
Large carrying capacity
Low trunk height
Electronic driver aids
Cruise control
Steering wheel controls

You can imagine a salesperson, having memorised these features, blandly reeling them off to a very bored customer, who may not be technically-minded nor understand what they all mean.

What the salesperson needs to do is go through feature lists and identify what benefit each feature gives a customer. It could look something like this:

Features	Benefits
2 Litre hybrid powered	Hybrid electric power supplements petrol engine reducing emissions, giving greater mileage, and saving fuel costs whilst maximising available power — all while not having to plug the car in to recharge.
Segregated air conditioning	Allows you and your passengers to set a temperature which suits each of you. No more arguments about the temperature in the car.
Alloy wheels	Look fantastic. Set you apart and are easier to clean.
Rear seat entertainment system	Keeps the kids entertained on those long journeys.
Panoramic sunroof	Lets the sun in and can be opened to let airflow through the car. Everything feels lighter and brighter.
Keyless entry	No more hunting through your pockets or purse looking for those keys when you return to your car laden with bags
Large carrying capacity	Great for shopping, carrying all your kids' sports equipment: fits 2 sets of golf clubs and a trolley.
Low trunk height	Makes lifting large objects into the trunk so much easier.
Electronic driver aids	Makes driving safer giving you peace of mind that in an emergency you have the best technology protecting you and your children.
Cruise control	Makes driving on those long journeys more relaxing. Arrive at your destination feeling fresh.
Steering wheel controls	You never have to take your hands off the wheel. No distractions. Everything is at hand.

Now, if we look at the list of features and benefits above, ask yourself 'what does the customer buy, features or benefits? The answer, of course, is that he buys benefits. He understands and can relate to the benefits even though he may not have understood the feature.

I have never understood why manufacturers list all the features of a product on the side of a box, yet they do not list the corresponding benefit. I am absolutely convinced that any manufacturer who did this would sell more product than the equivalent competitor who simply listed the features of their product.

Remember — a customer buys benefits, not features. So, let's go back to our salesperson selling the car. How do they get the benefits across to the customer? The answer as ever, is simple — by asking open questions and getting real, informative answers. The salesperson needs to identify which features would most benefit the customer and then highlighting them for the product.

What sports do your kids play? How much kit do you need to take to the practise field every week? If the answer is that they have a boy and a girl each playing different sports and they are running them to practise twice a week then having a trunk large enough is a great benefit which your customer will relate to.

What kind of journeys do you make in your vehicle? If the answer is that the customer likes to go on family road trips, then that rear entertainment system and even the segregated air conditioning is going to be a Godsend to them. Again, these benefits are real to the customer. They can relate to them. They can quantify them. They will buy them.

Are you getting the idea? It takes a few moments' thought with a sheet of blank paper to run through this exercise for any product. I urge you to try it now with your product, or if you do not have a product make one up but do go through the exercise.

List all the features in the left-hand column and then, in the right-hand column, their corresponding benefits.

Think about the 'open' questions you need to ask to get the customer to tell you the benefits that are most useful to her. After that, practise relating that benefit back to the corresponding feature of your product.

You will be absolutely amazed at how easy this process becomes once you have practised it a few times. You will rapidly catch yourself 'listing features' the next time you meet with a customer and realise how boring this sounds. Do not be a 'features seller', be a 'benefits seller' — they sell 10 times more!

In summary:

- Go through the exercise of linking benefits to the features of your product.
- Ask open questions to ascertain which benefits the customer needs.
- Practise this process until it becomes second nature.

8

Maximising Your Time

In every profession we have numerous tasks to complete throughout the day. Many are mundane, routine business housekeeping jobs that our managers insist we keep up with. We arrive in our office, make a coffee, catch up on last night's TV or sports event, then we meander to our desk and open our email, spending the next hour replying to or deleting the mundane emails that we receive every day. God forbid we open any social media application — there goes another hour!

The fact is that we can only sell to a customer when they are available. It is also a fact that we are more likely to progress a sale when that meeting is face to face even after the advent of Zoom, Skype, or Teams. Generally, this is 9 a.m. to 5 p.m. on a weekday. This is 'prime selling time' and you should maximise it.

Salespeople should break their day into specific tasks and organise accordingly:

- Customer Emails.
- Quotations.
- Updating customer records and making notes on where they are in the sales cycle.
- Internal company housekeeping.
- Travel time to meetings.
- Updating customer EDI systems and portals.
- Face to face meetings.
- Telephone calls (to progress the sale).

We should ask ourselves, which of the above tasks can only be carried out in 'Prime Selling Time'? The answer:

- Face to face meetings.
- Telephone calls (to progress the sale).

Everything else can be carried out outside of office time as far as humanly possible. In this way we maximise our available time with which to speak to or meet a customer. It follows that we maximise the time that we are *actually* selling.

In any sales training presentation I make, I always ask the attendees what percentage of their time is actually spent selling? I get various answers from 50% to 70%. In truth, for the average salesperson the answer is between 6% and 10%. If these 'average' salespeople are earning a reasonable salary whilst utilising 6–10% of their 'selling time', imagine what you could do if you double, treble, or quadruple that time!

Simply put, the more time you can allocate to progressing sales in Prime Selling Time then the more money you will earn. A professional salesperson building a business needs commitment. It is not a nine-to-five job if you want to be the best. The work-life balance will come later, but the hard work and long hours you put in now are what will get you there.

When I was a young salesperson, I stuck a note to my computer screen, and it simply read: 'IS THIS EARNING ME MONEY?' If I caught myself doing a task during 'Prime Selling Time' that was not progressing a sale (earning me money) then I immediately stopped doing it and refocussed on doing something that was. Try it, it is extremely motivating.

So how do we get organised? Well look at the tasks above and allow an hour before and/or an hour after 'Prime Selling Time' and complete those mundane tasks during those hours. Emails, quotations, updating records, internal company housekeeping, updating customer EDI systems and portals can all be done at that time.

For a meeting we must drive, ride a train, or fly to the customer. Whenever possible do this outside of 'Prime Selling Time'.

Organise your diary into daily blocks. If you have a customer meeting in a specific town, then book this on a future date and then contact all your other customers in that area so you can see them on the same day. Drive up early in the morning, start your first meeting at 9 a.m. and then work your route to see 4, maybe 5 other customers or potential customers on the same day. Maximise your time.

Block book another day or half day to make customer calls which progress them through the sales cycle. Block book another day to make new customer calls. Remember we must keep feeding the pipeline, otherwise our current sales pipeline runs down (we lose or win deals) and if we have not fed new customers into the pipeline, we will hit a slump in sales. This is not good for you or the company you work for.

Ask yourself this: when was the last time you said the words, 'Hello, you don't know me, my name is Joe. Can you give me 5 minutes of your time so that I can introduce myself and my company?' Ask yourself this question every day. If the answer is that it has been a while, then block book a day in your diary the following week to speak to new customers. This is imperative to your success as a salesperson.

Your calendar is your bible. It should be with you wherever you go whether it is a manual calendar, an electronic calendar, or part of your CRM system. As you meet a customer or speak to a customer, you should make a forward note to call that customer again on one of your 'blocked for calls' days in the future. In this way three things will happen: (1) You will never miss a follow up call with that customer, (2) You will maximise your time progressing customers through your sales cycle, and (3) You will retain control of the sales process.

After every meeting and every phone call you have two tasks:

1. Make a note of the conversation you had and what the next agreed steps with that customer are.
2. Put a note in your diary for the next meeting date or the next time you need to call that customer.

This system becomes imperative once you have built an active sales pipeline. Let's say you have 50 customers 'in pipeline'. Your day will be extraordinarily busy. You will feel like you are juggling plates! By being organised and block booking your time you will never let one fall and maximise your use of 'Prime Selling Time'.

In summary:

- Identify the different functions within your role.
- Reserve prime selling time to the functions which involve contact with your customers.
- Block book your calendar to maximise your time.
- Book forward follow up calls and meetings for every customer, so you never lose control of the process.
- Ask yourself, 'Is this earning me money?'

9

Types of Meeting

Every time you meet or speak to a customer you need to understand and plan what your objectives are for that meeting. You also need an understanding of what your customer is trying to achieve in talking to you. There are essentially 5 types of meeting that we have as salespeople:

1. Cold Introduction.
2. Known Introduction.
3. Presentation.
4. Confirmation/Sales Cycle movement.
5. Closing meeting.

Cold Introduction

This meeting (or phone call) is with a prospective customer that we have not spoken to before. As such, you will need to ask open questions to find out if he has a problem which your product can solve. You need background and information so you can provide him with the best possible solution. Here are the objectives for this type of meeting:

- Agree on an agenda.
- Establish credibility.
- Gain information.
- Build rapport.
- Establish the customer's interest.
- Qualify:
  - the person.
  - the company.

- Establish a path to move forward.
- Summarise the meeting.

Known Introduction

This meeting (or phone call) is with a prospective customer that we have not spoken to before but essentially, we are known to him. This could be a lead gained from an exhibition. He could have made an inquiry to your website. You could have been recommended to him by a friend or business colleague. This meeting is similar to a cold introduction but perhaps can be viewed a little more positively and you can achieve your objectives a little easier as the customer has already expressed an interest in you and your products. Here are the objectives for this type of meeting:

- Agree on an agenda.
- Reaffirm credibility.
- Build rapport.
- Establish needs.
- Outline your solution.
- Qualify:
  - the person.
  - the company.
- Gain information.
- Establish a path to move forward.
- Summarise the meeting.

Presentation

This meeting is with a prospective customer that is already in pipeline and usually at the 'prove' stage. This is your opportunity to show the customer that your solution is the right one for him. Objectives for this meeting are as follows:

- State your objective today.
- Establish corporate and personal credibility.

- Establish a solution (prove the product).
- Create an impact.
- Create a path forwards.
- Retain control of the sale at this crucial stage.

The customer presentation meeting is so important and so powerful for a salesperson that there is a whole chapter devoted to the subject next.

Sales cycle Movement/Confirmation Meeting

This meeting or phone call has one overriding objective which is to move the customer along your sales cycle (and ensure that you understand where he is on his buying cycle). It may be that you are identifying his exact requirements ready to prepare a quotation, it may be that he has tested your product, and you want to ensure that your solution has been 'proved' by the customer. It may be a discussion to ascertain that he has approved his budget for the deal.

Depending on these things you will need to prepare carefully for this meeting and potentially involve other people from your company or your customer's. If your contact is not the only person involved in the buying process (it may need to be signed off by the Managing Director) then you must do your best to make sure that all the relevant people are in the meeting.

One of the first things you will have established with the customer is if he alone has the authority to make the purchase from you. Some salespeople can find this embarrassing to ask and indeed, some buyers do not like to admit that they alone do not have the authority to make a buying decision! An easy solution is to ask the customer, "Who, apart from yourself, will be involved in this buying decision?" By asking this question you have made the customer aware that you know he is important, and you will not be undermining his authority if you need to speak to someone else who may be involved in their buying process. If someone else is involved in the decision to buy, they must be in this meeting.

Here is an outline of the objectives you need to think about:

- Agree on an agenda.
- Confirm previous agreements.
- Qualify customer's position.
- Gain further and updated information.
- Establish a path to move forward.
- Summarise the meeting.

Closing Meeting

This meeting is all about getting the deal and your customer placing an order. There is nothing fancy to do here. You have one objective. It is very simple:

- Ask for the order.

If you have done your job and closed every step along the sales cycle. If your customer has been through their buying cycle, simply ask your customer for an order.

In summary:

- Understand the type of meeting you are about to conduct.
- Set your objectives and understand your customer's objectives.
- Get your customer's agreement and summarise the meeting.
- Establish the next step.
- Retain control.

10

Presentations

Every time you get an opportunity to make a stand-up presentation to a customer (or possibly his department) grab it with both hands. A presentation opportunity can come at the beginning of the sales cycle (introducing yourself to the customer) or much better halfway through the sales cycle at the 'proving' stage.

At this point you will have had conversations with the customer that have established their problem, their budget, their timescale. You will have established credibility with the customer and be well on your way to getting the sale. The bit that has not yet been achieved is that you need to 'prove' your solution works and that it will meet the customer's needs (solve their problem).

Having asked the customer, 'Who else, apart from yourself, is involved in the buying process?' it may be that there are several people needing to be convinced that your solution is the right one. Those people might be engineers, technicians, finance people, management, or more senior buyers. You need to identify who will be there, why they are there and ascertain if you need backup resources from your own company to attend also. If you are presenting a technical software solution for example, it may be a good idea to have your implementation manager and a product expert at the meeting ready to answer any technical questions which may arise.

Suggesting at this stage that you present your solution to the customer group is an excellent idea. For me, as a professional salesperson, I can tell you that in my career, if the customer agreed to a presentation from me (with all the relevant decision makers present), my chances of winning that deal were much higher.

Making a stand-up presentation gives you the opportunity to demonstrate your product in a controlled environment, or better still, getting your own technical expert to demonstrate the product for you. This means the customer might need to only carry out negligible testing themselves or even none to pass the 'prove' stage.

In a stand-up presentation, you are in control of the agenda. You can set the path forward and look at each person around the table and get their individual agreement. You are standing up (sometimes with a microphone) and therefore you control the room. If someone asks a question which is awkward (or not relevant) you can ask them to leave questions to the end of the presentation or you can suggest they have a side-bar meeting later with your technical manager.

In short, you have complete control. With every decision maker in the room, you can individually speak to them and ascertain and answer their personal objections. Answering and overcoming them in that environment (in front of everyone) gives the buyer you are dealing with de-facto permission to go ahead with the purchase.

You should leave your presentation having created an impact, showing the customer that your solution works and will work for them and having everyone in that room agreeing with the next steps which need to be taken to close the sale.

If you have little experience in delivering presentations, do try to get some training in this area. It is the most powerful sales tool in your arsenal. Get as much practise as you can. You will become more comfortable standing and speaking in front of a group of people and once you have understood and experienced the impact it can have on your sales success you will want to use it more and more in helping you move through the sales cycle with a customer.

A few tips:

- Never put a PowerPoint presentation up and read what is written on the slides. The people watching can read for themselves. Put simple, concise bullet points on the slide, pause and allow the audience to read them and then speak around those points to get across the point you are making.
- Make eye contact with everyone in the room. Practise by scanning the room left to right and back again.
- Lift your chin up and project your voice to the back of the room.
- Do not be afraid to step forward from your position on a podium or stage. By stepping forward and getting closer to the audience you will grab and retain their attention. Do not hide behind a podium.
- Know your stuff. Understand before you start what you are going to say. Be ready and have answers ready for questions. If you do not know technical answers always refer those questions to a colleague with you who can answer correctly.
- Understand who you are talking to. Is English their first language? If not, slow your voice down and speak very clearly. Ensure they understand. Nod at them and they will nod back!
- When you practise your presentation, do so by speaking out loud. You will be amazed how different it sounds out loud (rather than just thinking the words over silently in your head).
- Do not have anything in your hands. Your hands speak as much as your voice. If you use a pen to write on a white board for example, put it down afterwards.
- Small cue cards are OK but they should be just that — a cue for your next point. Never have the presentation written in

long hand for you to read out. If you're using a well-made slideshow, the bullet points can act as your cue.

- Achieve your objective.

In summary:

- Presentations are powerful tools for you.
- Make sure every relevant person is present.
- Be prepared as far as possible.
- Practise public and group speaking as often as possible.
- Control the proceedings.

11

Forecasting and Reviewing

Why do we forecast? Well, there are several good reasons. You will find that the management within the company you work for requires a reasonable estimation of the sales that are going to be closed over the next 1, 3, 6 or 12 months. Their function is to ensure that the company is geared up to supply the expected orders and that there are the necessary resources in place to meet those orders. Secondly, you, as a professional salesperson need an estimation of your future earnings and performance. You will have already been through the exercise of working out how much you want to earn. That's all well and good, but you need to track your performance very regularly to ensure that you are on course to reach your personal earnings target.

Your forecast has a profound effect on the business you work for. Senior managers will be taking decisions based on your estimation of future orders: the raw materials they must forward buy, the number of staff they need to recruit, and the size of warehouse they need to occupy. Do they need to open a new production line to meet demand? Do they need to close a product line that is no longer selling?

Because these decisions will have such an effect on the company and indeed, on people's lives, forecasting is often fraught with anxiety, especially for a young salesperson who has little or no experience of the process. Salespeople are at the 'sharp' end of the business. They are responsible for generating orders and therefore generating cash for the company. Often, they are the department that feels most pressure and the environment can become pressurised if not stressful. If they do not perform or bring in what they forecast, then this is highly visible to the whole company, piling on more pressure.

For all these reasons, I have yet to meet a salesperson that welcomed the forecasting process. Working in sales is hectic every day. Because you are the contact point for the customer you will find that your time is limited and mostly taken up with the task of moving your prospects through the sales cycle. For you, this is the most important and profitable way to spend your time. For the managers and colleagues in other departments who are relying on your forecast (and its accuracy) however, forecasting takes on a higher priority. Arriving at the end of the month and having to assess every deal in your pipeline to 'come up with a guestimate number' often with a manager breathing over your shoulder, is simply not professional.

So how do we make the process simple, efficient, accurate, and most importantly, not allow it to take up too much of your time? The answer is to use the Denham Method of sales and visually represent that on the page or screen. You will have a working copy of your forecast that is updated constantly as you speak to customers and move them through the sales cycle. This can be done with a very simple Excel spreadsheet or via a suitable Customer Relationship Management (CRM) program.

At the end of each working day this is updated. At the end of the month, you can 'fix' a copy of this forecast and simply hand it to your manager. The columns can be adjusted by size of deal, month in which the order is due or by the probability of you closing the deal. This gives your management a fair representation of the sales pipeline that you are currently working on.

Regarding the probability of you getting the deal, you can use the following ratios. As the customer moves through the sales cycle, the probability of you winning the business gets better. As you translate this to your forecast sheet you can sort the spreadsheet to show the highest probability deals within a given month.

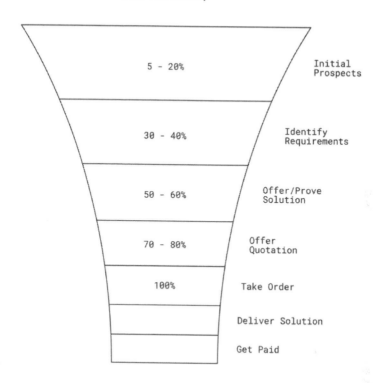

Deal Probability

5 - 20%   Initial
               Prospects

30 - 40%   Identify
               Requirements

50 - 60%   Offer/Prove
               Solution

70 - 80%   Offer
               Quotation

100%   Take Order

               Deliver Solution

               Get Paid

A typical sales forecast consists of a single spreadsheet with customer names listed in the left column and stages of the sales cycle listed across the document. It should include an 'order due' column which is the estimated date that the order will come in. It should also have a 'deal value' column which can be amended as the deal goes through sales cycle.

As you amend this document day to day, you can simply update the estimated dates of sales cycle movement and even update the value of the deal as your ongoing discussions with the customer affect your proposal. You add new customers to the forecast as they are introduced to your pipeline.

The forecast should be fixed and reviewed every month. Your manager, once presented with this document, should be able to compare it to the previous months' forecasts and easily see what has moved through the sales cycle and perhaps which deals have stalled. They can easily see that you are growing the value of your pipeline and that you are on target to reach your annual goals.

You should not regard the forecasting process as a test. Indeed, these numbers are never cast in stone. This is a fixed, snapshot version of a live document which changes every day. In this way it is the most accurate and up to date visual of your pipeline that is easily understood and, when compared to previous forecasts shows your progress for anyone to understand.

Once your manager understands the Denham Method of sales that you are using, she can use this snapshot to help and advise you on individual deals. Let's say she spots that a deal has stalled, and no updates have been made from the previous forecast. Perhaps she can offer to visit the customer with you to lend some weight to your proposal with that customer. As a salesperson you often feel solely responsible for winning or losing a deal. You should never be afraid to call upon support resources within the business to help you move a deal forward. This forecast enables your manager to have a discussion with you about individual deals and gives you the chance to discuss support you need.

When having a monthly sales update meeting with my sales staff, I would often be able to offer help and guidance to the salesperson even to the point where (with the salesperson's permission) we would call the customer together and confirm the customer's position and thoughts on our proposal. The fact that a more senior person has called him and taken a personal interest in his business often has a very positive effect and pushes the customer through the sales cycle. I would urge you to work with your manager in this way. It is an excellent team approach and gives a superior impression of your company.

It is also important that you can take the decision to give up on any deal that is less likely to happen. You have seen that you will win only 20% or 1 in 5 deals that go into your pipeline. As salespeople we always find it difficult to let a deal go, but you must do this as your time is limited and you need to maximise this time to work on the deals that are more likely to close. I suggest that you take those decisions in your monthly discussion with your manager. Taking the decision together with a senior manager will give you the confidence to concentrate on the deals you feel have the highest chance of closing. In this way you will maximise the revenue you generate for your business and your earnings.

Forecasting should never be a chore. It should never take up more than a few minutes of your time. It should be an accurate, real-time representation of the customers you have in your pipeline at that moment. You should also regularly read and discuss it with your manager so that they can easily see where you are in your pipeline growth and more importantly, how they can assist you with any resources you need to help you win more business. If you follow the Denham Method, forecasting is automatic, real-time, accurate, and easy.

In summary:

- Update your forecast at the end of every day in real time.
- Give every deal a current probability and update this every time you speak to the customer.
- Do not be afraid to erase a potential deal from your forecast. You must concentrate on the deals that will happen. Take these decisions with your manager.
- Compare your fixed monthly forecast to last month's. What moved through sales cycle? What did not? Why?
- Call upon company resources to help you move a deal through sales cycle if you need to.

12

A Different Way to Set Targets

Targets are a wonderful thing — especially when you have a bonus payable once the target has been reached!

It is important that you sit with the senior managers of the business that you work for and agree an annual sales target with them. You should not simply have an arbitrary target imposed on you that you have not discussed.

The target should be reasonable. It should be ambitious but achievable. Giving a salesperson an unachievable target is a mortal business sin in my opinion. It is simply demotivating. Should you find yourself working for a manager or company that insists on setting unrealistic targets then the best way to push back is as follows. Suggest setting 3 separate target levels. Let's say they want to set your target at an unrealistic $150K sales per month ($1.8m annual), then you should suggest 3 target levels as follows:

T1 Minimum	$100K pm	$1.2m annual
T2 Acceptable	$120K pm	$1.44m annual
T3 Incredible	$150K pm	$1.8m annual

Negotiate a bonus on achieving the acceptable and an exceptional bonus on achieving the incredible result. Remember that once you have achieved annual sales that exceed the company's break-even figure for employing you, then any sales above this level are more profitable for the company. They can afford to pay you a bonus for achieving exceptional sales and indeed, should be encouraged to do so.

I would also urge caution in your annual target negotiation if you have had an exceptional year in sales. The company will look at what you achieved the year before and automatically treat this level of sales as the new bar by which you are measured. If it was an exceptional year do point that out and keep the target for the following year realistic.

Many companies do not pay an annual bonus on achieving target. This is quite normal. Just be sure that the OTE (on target earnings) figure that you set is acceptable to you and that you are confident in achieving it.

Revenue targets are important and give you tremendous confidence when you achieve them and move through your sales career. However, they are not the be-all and end-all of measuring sales success. As a professional salesperson you are dedicated, hardworking and committed to achieving success. You are a driven individual. For me this did not just mean achieving my set revenue targets. Other types of business sales goals you could set yourself include:

- Adding 10 new customers to your pipeline every month.
- Looking at a geographical area where you currently do not do business and bringing in customers from there.
- Achieving a certain number of sales every month regardless of value.
- Establishing a new product and introducing it to your pipeline.
- Giving yourself a mini target value of repeat sales to existing customers.
- Increasing the 'close' ratio of business introduced into pipeline from 20% to 25%.

I set myself more individual goals and they gave me the impetus to drive forward and push myself even harder.

I cannot tell you what your personal goals are, so in this section I am going to give some examples of the type of goals which will motivate you like no other. At some point in my life these all applied to me. For me, aside from my company revenue targets, I sat down at the beginning of the year and created goals that I wanted to achieve with the next 3 months and goals that I wanted to achieve that year.

It is also imperative that you write these goals down and review them every 3 months. Just as you do with your sales target review, you should review your personal goals and note: Which goals did you achieve? Which goals did you not achieve? Why?

You do not have to share your personal goals with anyone, but I would urge you to write them down and review them with yourself. It is an exercise in being truthful with yourself and your own ambitions. We all start with the best intentions in the world, but achievement (breeding confidence) cannot be attained without self-motivation. Here are some ideas:

Quarterly goals

- Buy a new outfit.
- Take up a new hobby.
- Have a long weekend away.
- Have dinner at the restaurant that you always wanted to try.

Annual goals

- Buy a new car.
- Learn to play guitar.
- Save the deposit for a house purchase.
- Get engaged.
- Get married.
- Visit that dream destination.
- Plan to have children.
- Get a pet!

Write down your goals, review whether you achieved them. Do not beat yourself up if you did not, life is a marathon not a sprint. If, in your mind, you associate your personal goals with your sales profession you will give yourself the motivation to succeed.

Remember, nobody owes you anything in life. Learn how to self-motivate. It is the most powerful tool you have to achieve great things.

In summary:

- Agree to ambitious but achievable targets.
- Set different business goals, not just revenue targets.
- Set personal, achievable goals and write them down.
- Constantly review your business and personal goals.

13

Territory and Customer Management

Territory management is all about planning. As a new salesperson you will be given a territory within which your company wants you to extract the maximum sales. This territory could be geographical, and it could be a large or small area depending on your product and market. It may be that you have the whole of the UK to ply your trade, or you could be limited to a few counties.

Alternatively, your territory could be outlined by a type of customer. So, a company could employ one salesperson to sell to all insurance companies and another to sell to banks. This tends to be the case if, for example, you are selling a technical software product into the market. Specialist industry knowledge would be most important in this instance. An insurance company has very different considerations than a bank. You would be expected to learn and have intimate knowledge of the companies that you are targeting and their systems and processes.

In either case, it is important that you understand the target market that you have been assigned. Ensure that there is no ambiguity when it comes to stating the market segment you have been assigned.

Once this has been established, you can start to plan your approach to the market. Firstly, look at the overall market potential. How many potential customers sit within your territory? Let's say you identify 8,000 potential customers; you can then compare this to your average sale value and the number of sales you need to achieve your goals. If you need to make 10 sales per month, then, in your territory you need to achieve a market penetration of 1.5% of the available customers. To achieve this, you need to be introducing 600 of those potential customers into your pipeline.

This may sound daunting, but the secret is to break everything down into small steps and build your business progressively. 600 customers equate to just 50 per month. Use your company's marketing resource to generate leads. Can they invest in a marketing email campaign or a social media campaign outlining the benefits of your product and perhaps then generating inquiries which go straight into pipeline as 'known introductions'.

You can easily obtain a list of your potential customers with contacts and telephone numbers. Google search is your friend and often industry trade associations will have a database of companies or members who fit the category of customer you are looking for. LinkedIn is also an excellent tool to research companies and the people who work in them.

Make sure you understand who within your target organisation you are selling to. What role within the company is going to buy your product. If you are selling building maintenance equipment, then you need to identify building maintenance managers. If you are selling IT solutions, you need to identify the IT manager who is responsible for purchases within the organisation. This may sound obvious but often companies allocate responsibilities very differently. Call them and ask open questions: 'Who do I need to speak to in your organisation that is responsible for purchasing toilet rolls?' You are starting at the beginning of your sales journey. Identifying the correct person to speak to is paramount in your success.

As the business landscape changes and that rate of change accelerates, businesses need to keep up with the latest market innovations to ensure the ongoing success and growth of their businesses. Some industry knowledge (gained by research) is essential to your ability to maximise your time and target the customers most likely to buy.

Within your market there will be innovators and followers. The innovators are out there pushing for the latest technology or product which will give them a competitive edge. They are most likely to invest in new ideas and new products as they become available. The followers will wait, bide their time, and see how successful a new product has been with a competitor first. If it is a success they will invest later and install the new system or buy the product with far less risk of it going wrong for them. If you can identify the innovators and followers in your marketplace and you have a new, innovative product to sell, then far better to target the innovators in the early days.

It is important to note that in the life cycle of any product, there is always a primary demand from the innovators, followed by a secondary demand which will truly establish the product in the marketplace and then there is a period of growth where the product is readily proven and more easily recognised and purchased.

At this research and planning stage you must look at the competition. Which other companies and products are you going to be competing against? How do they compare to you and your products? Are they more expensive? Cheaper? Lower quality? Made from a different material? Do your research and imagine yourself offering a quotation to a customer in competition with this other product or company. Where do you have the edge? What benefits can you emphasise to the customer which will set you apart from the competition?

Once you are committed and you have this competitive knowledge then go about your business with confidence and passion. In my career, once my initial research was done, I very rarely worried about competition. I had the best product and my passion for matching that product to the customers who would most benefit from my solution was enough to win the business. Many salespeople fall into the trap of obsessing about competitive products. Never do this. You can acknowledge that they exist, but your product is better so why worry?

The last point I will make on territory management is that you must have the management of your company working with you to ensure that the product you are selling complies with the territory you are selling into. You would be amazed how some companies with products that sell well in the UK decide to expand their horizons and employ a salesperson to sell that product into a new market without checking these points. Before you take that sales job, make sure that the product complies with the new market requirements. Do they have the correct licensing agreements in place? Do they comply with the government regulations within the new territory? Are the packaging and instructions available in the correct language? Do they understand the geography of the new territory and have the logistical support in place to deliver the product in a timely and efficient manner?

A good example of this is expanding your sales into Canada. You may have been successfully selling your product in North America and see Canada as an easy low hanging fruit to expand into. It is the law in Canada that packaging of any retail product is not only displayed in English but also in French Canadian. Not only that, the wording of both languages on the packaging must be of equal size and the same font. You need to understand these things before you go about a sales drive into a new territory.

Once you have done your market and territory research and generated a sales pipeline within a territory, you will start to win business and build a loyal customer base over the coming months and years. Your product may be one which has a limited life and need to be replaced, or it may be that once you have established business with that customer, he will continually buy from you. Perhaps your product is a component of a product he is producing, or he is even reselling your products. It is at this point that your role slightly changes, and you need to distinguish between 'new business' sales and 'existing customer account management'.

Some companies even split these roles out and employ new business salespeople and account managers whose role is to look after existing customers. Often there will be a significant difference in sales commission rates between these roles. New business will command a higher rate of commission.

The majority of what we have covered so far in this book relates to winning new business. Once you have established a customer you may then be expected to look after and re-sell to them on a regular basis. You must take this into account when you are organising your time. Depending on your product you must make time to visit existing customers regularly, ensure that your solution is still relevant and find out if they have new needs that you can meet. Of course, your goal here is to create an ongoing working relationship that benefits you and your customer.

What you must not do at this point is neglect bringing in new business on a regular basis. Remember to keep introducing new prospects to your sales pipeline. If you rely on existing business for most of your income, then you can get caught out if that customer decides to stop purchasing from you. This can happen for any number of reasons which are outside of your control. Ensure that you are maximising your time with an eye on serving your existing customers and winning new business.

By now you will have ascertained that organisation is very much a key part in your success as a salesperson. With the advent of computer applications to assist us in our daily work it has become so much easier to manage our day-to-day lives using incredibly powerful tools on our computers. Forward planning in your calendar and the ability to invite people to meetings with automated calendar entries is so normal now that people do not even comment on it. For you as a salesperson, understanding how these basic applications work and how they can help you to be as organised as you can be is imperative.

There is so much training available online for you to get the most out of the most basic applications, I would urge you to take advantage of this. For you to have a complete understanding of Word, Excel, Outlook, and other basic applications is imperative to maximising your time and income as a salesperson.

The most important organisation tool in your armoury is the customer relationship management (CRM) system you use. This is a database application that allows you to input your prospect and customer contact details and then record your ongoing correspondence with that customer. It also allows you to make timely notes and record what was said in phone calls and meetings. Some of the more sophisticated CRM systems allow you to create a graphic representation of your pipeline and see in real time where every one of your customers is within the sales cycle. This of course replaces the manual spreadsheet example that I showed you in Chapter 11.

There are many CRM systems out there. The most famous and biggest is almost certainly Salesforce. Then you have HubSpot, Zoho, Pipedrive, Insightly and many, many others. I have used most of these at one time or another and in truth, I have never found one yet that has entirely satisfied my needs as a salesperson. They are always a compromise. The best ones are the simplest in my view. What you want is the CRM system that you will use daily and not get frustrated with. Much will depend on your company's existing CRM system or whether they are able to invest in one. They can be very expensive.

If your company does not have a CRM and cannot afford that investment, then you should consider using a combination of standard products to write notes and forecast. A combination of Excel, Word and Outlook Calendar will do what a CRM essentially does. It will just not have some of the fancy reporting and tools that a CRM system has.

It is imperative that you take notes after every meeting or phone call especially as you get busier and your sales pipeline grows. There is no doubt that once you reach a certain number of customers you will forget some details or follow up calls.

Using the Denham Method and forward booking your follow up calls should alleviate this, but use of a good CRM system is incredibly helpful.

You do not have to write an essay after each customer contact. A few sentences and notes to yourself should be sufficient to jog your memory next time you speak to the customer. It is always good to give yourself personal notes. It may be that your customer was planning on going on a big holiday after your meeting. Make a note of this and be sure to ask them how their holiday was next time you speak to them. This personal interest in your customer is immensely important in establishing your customer relationship. It should also be genuine and relevant. I have made hundreds of friends with customers over the years. Remember, people buy from people, and it is important that you take an interest in your customers.

Modern CRM systems can incorporate research and marketing tools and can become way more than a simple central customer database application. Systems that can scour the internet and let you know what your competition is up to, what marketing trends and keywords are coming to the fore can assist a company in their marketing program. As a professional salesperson I am more inclined to leave the marketing side of the business to the marketing department and maximise my time with the inquiries that they produce. Keep your life simple and extremely well organised.

In summary:

- Agree your territory and research it thoroughly.
- Get organised. Adopt and use a CRM or do it manually with other software applications.
- Feed new customers into the pipeline very regularly.
- Make notes after every customer contact.

14

Electronic Data Interchange (EDI) Systems

In the ever-evolving landscape of sales and commerce, staying competitive requires embracing technology. One of the most powerful tools at your disposal is Electronic Data Interchange, or EDI. This chapter explores the world of EDI and how it can supercharge your sales efforts.

Electronic Data Interchange is a method of exchanging business documents electronically in a standardized format. These documents can include purchase orders, invoices, shipping notifications, and more. EDI systems enable businesses to communicate seamlessly, reducing the need for manual data entry, and paper documents.

If, for example you are selling products into a major retail chain, they will almost certainly require you to communicate with them through an EDI system. This is usually a third-party company like SPS Commerce who will facilitate the connection and interchange of documents between your company and the retailer.

Why is this important to you as a salesperson? Your orders will no longer arrive attached to an email. They will be automatically placed within the EDI system and input to your company's accounting system. You will need to be able to access regular reports from the system to understand and confirm that the orders you are expecting from your customer are arriving correctly and that the details on the orders are also correct.

Your input to the setup of the system is imperative to the success of the interchange. You will need to input your product details into the system and ensure that everything you input is correct and then updated regularly.

Choosing the right EDI system is key and must integrate with your existing company software. Usually, your customer will give you a choice of one or two systems that they currently use. Whatever system is chosen, you must ensure that you and the relevant staff within your organisation are well trained and that the integration is well tested before 'going live'. It should seamlessly integrate with your current sales and inventory management tools.

It can often seem that your job as a salesperson has changed focus rapidly once you have initiated an EDI setup with your customer. However, the basic tenets of sales practise should never be forgotten, and you must remember that you are still dealing with a buyer on the other side of the system. Any price updates or product changes must be made within the system and the customer must be made aware and agree to them.

An EDI system, when set up correctly, will benefit you in many ways. Traditional sales transactions often involve a lot of back-and-forth communication, which can be time-consuming. With EDI these transactions can happen in real-time, reducing delays and accelerating the sales process. Manual data entry is prone to errors, which can lead to costly mistakes and miscommunication. EDI eliminates this risk by automating data transfer, ensuring accuracy and consistency.

Reducing the need for paper documents, postage, and manual labour can result in significant cost savings. EDI streamlines operations, ultimately making your business more profitable. This has the added benefit of being more environmentally friendly. As a professional salesperson you should welcome the EDI system, as it will enable quick response times and accurate order processing, which should lead to increased customer satisfaction. Happy customers are more likely to become repeat buyers.

When first faced with an EDI setup, it can be very daunting. Take best advice from your customer and the EDI company. Get as much help as you can within your organisation and get the buy-in from staff that will need to ensure the smooth operation of the system. EDI can give your business a competitive edge. Embrace this technology, and you'll be well on your way to a more profitable and streamlined sales process.

In summary:

- Test any EDI setup rigorously before going live.
- Take care to input product and price information correctly.
- Check and update the EDI system information regularly.
- Ensure that you and other relevant staff in the company are trained and understand the EDI system.
- Remember there is a real buyer on the other side of the EDI system. Do not neglect them.

15

Marketplace Selling

Many traditional brick-and-mortar retailers are now looking to establish not just consumer sales websites but also 'marketplace' platforms. Amazon, Wayfair, and eBay are the major marketplaces in operation, but we are now seeing Walmart, Macey's, John Lewis, and most major retailers developing their own platforms.

What is a 'marketplace'? With a marketplace, any supplier can apply to list their products for sale on the platform. You can choose from several delivery and logistics options, perhaps allowing the marketplace to centrally stock and deliver your products (e.g., Fulfilled By Amazon (FBA) on Amazon) or choosing a 'dropship' option. With dropshipping, once the consumer places an order, that order is passed to you (minus the retailer's margin) and you then have the responsibility of delivering your product directly to the consumer.

Selling on these platforms can be a very lucrative business strategy especially if you have a unique product and a recognisable brand, but there is no shortcut to success. Success on marketplace platforms often takes time and patience. It's essential to continuously learn and adapt your strategy based on the ever-changing dynamics of e-commerce. Building a solid presence and reputation on these platforms takes time and continual monitoring to succeed.

Research before you jump in with both feet is key. Understand the specific rules, policies, and fees of the marketplace platform you're targeting. Each platform has unique requirements and guidelines, so you need to adapt your strategy accordingly. Select the platform that aligns with your product niche and target audience. Different platforms cater to different demographics and product categories, so pick the one that best fits your business.

Create compelling product listings with high-quality images, detailed descriptions, and competitive pricing. Use relevant keywords to improve search visibility on the platform. There is a huge amount of information available from the major platforms and you should take their training and follow their instructions. They know what works. They have the data to confirm it and they want you to succeed. Pricing plays a crucial role in your success. Monitor your competitors' prices and offer competitive, yet profitable, pricing for your products.

Make sure you understand all the fees being charged by the marketplace. Chargebacks, marketing fees, storage costs, returns charges, and management fees all add up. Before you list any product, make sure you understand the fees and that you are still making a reasonable profit yourself.

Provide excellent customer service. Respond promptly to customer inquiries and address issues or concerns. Positive reviews and ratings can significantly impact your sales. Customers from around the world in different time zones need to be made aware of your response times and these need to be as fast as possible.

One of the key reasons that your forecasting is so important is that in e-commerce business, your inventory management is imperative. Stocks need to be maintained to avoid running out of popular items. On the other hand, avoid overstocking to prevent unnecessary storage costs. If you continually run out of stock on an item that sells well, some marketplaces will punish you by reducing your visibility on the platform. It will also affect their forecasts of sales of your product and make it very much more difficult for you to have forward visibility of how many products you need to supply in the coming months.

Over time, work on building a brand presence within the marketplace. This can help you gain customer trust and loyalty. You can build towards having your own branded shop within the marketplace, which can be a very lucrative long-term strategy. As you grow your presence, consider offering a variety of related products within your niche to appeal to a broader customer base and increase cross-selling opportunities.

This is a very fast-moving sales environment, and it is incredibly competitive. Marketplace platforms frequently update their rules and algorithms. Stay informed about these changes and adapt your strategy accordingly. Constant monitoring of the marketplace environment, competition, and pricing is very important if you want to stay ahead of the game and continually succeed with a long-term strategy. As your sales grow, be prepared to scale your operations. This may involve optimizing your supply chain, improving customer support, and expanding your product line.

In my experience, the data offered to you as a supplier from the major platforms is excellent. Regularly review sales data, customer feedback, and platform analytics. Use this information to make data-driven decisions and adapt your strategy. Platforms like Amazon and Wayfair are built and driven by data. They know what customers are searching for, where those customers are located, and when those customers are likely to buy. They will feed this information back to you, so you need to ensure that you apply your marketing skills to take advantage of this. Spending advertising and promotion money on the platform at the right time is key to your success.

Use the platform's advertising tools to promote your products. Paid ads, promotions, and discounts can help increase visibility and sales. This needs care and attention, and it is so important to the success of your marketplace business that I have expanded on this subject in the next chapter.

In summary:

- Research the platform before committing to it.
- Understand the costs you will be charged.
- Create compelling product listings.
- Provide excellent customer service.
- Update inventory numbers regularly.
- Do not run out of popular items.
- Build a brand presence.
- Keep up with marketplace changes.
- Review the data, understand it and change strategy if necessary.

16

Social Media and the Advent of Retail Media

In my last business, which I ran from 2009 to 2023, I very rarely resorted to legacy print advertising. The marketing of the business was built around the core social media platforms. We made best use of Instagram, Facebook, and Pinterest for our branded consumer-facing marketing, and this was very successful.

A consumer magazine that circulates to 60,000 people would charge many thousands of dollars for a full or half page advertisement for your product. Readers of the magazine may or may not read your advertisement and they may or may not respond to it. A response of 0.5 percent of that 60,000 people would be an excellent result.

With Facebook or Instagram, you can define who you want to reach, and those platforms have the data to tell you who is interested in your product. If you are selling gardening gloves for example, and your typical customer is female and aged 35–60, Facebook will know who fits that demographic within a specific geographical area and they will also know the people within that demographic who are perhaps interested in gardening. They may be in a group or subscribe to a page that shows that interest. For just a few cents per impression you can get your advertisement in front of those exact people. This is incredibly powerful and is akin to 'rifle shot' marketing as opposed to the 'shotgun' approach of traditional advertising.

As a professional salesperson, you need to be aware of and have input into the social media campaigns that your company is carrying out. A consumer-facing social media campaign can be a powerful lead and sales generation machine. You need to couple this with offers and promotions into your retailers which match and support those promotions.

When selling to a retailer, especially when you first start doing business, you can use geo-targeting tools within social media to drive consumers to that retail store where they can now find your product. A buyer within the retail shop is much more likely to stock your product if you are providing a campaign that will generate immediate sales. An initial campaign that gets your sales moving in that shop is a powerful tool in your sales arsenal and is relatively inexpensive.

What we have seen in the last 20 years is a massive change in the way advertising works. Google pioneered the change with the advent of 'Google AdWords'. For a few cents you could bid on a key word or phrase and when a consumer searched that phrase you would be placed at the top of the search giving you an exponentially greater chance of the customer clicking onto your listing. This was and continues to be very powerful and lucrative.

We then saw Facebook enter the marketplace and use their massive knowledge of their users' likes and personal data to be able to package that knowledge into a 'rifle shot' advertising package for sellers. It has the edge over AdWords in that Facebook knows what the user is interested in on an everyday basis. Targeting in this way is incredibly powerful and gives the advertiser a far greater return for their advertising dollars.

Social media brand promotion and awareness is very inexpensive. When a company puts together a successful brand campaign and couples this with rifle-shot advertising on the platform you can generate interest, sales and growth on a scale and timescale that has never before been available.

Alongside this, we have seen social media move into the 'influencer' stage. Major global influencers can now earn millions of dollars per post because they can reach millions of people instantly with a positive endorsement of a product. Even minor influencers can reach hundreds of thousands of people instantly. No traditional magazine advertisement can do that.

The latest advertising innovation is in 'Retail Media' and this is a phrase that you, as a professional salesperson will hear more and more. It relates to retailers and particularly marketplace retailers demanding that you advertise on their platform for you to get a higher place in their listings and therefore achieve more sales. Retail media incorporates several elements:

- Reviews.
- Advertising.
- Promotions.

It is very important that you understand these elements, what effect they have, and when it is best to spend money on them. When you sign up to a marketplace like Amazon or Wayfair you will list your product and then be deluged with information and offers to run promotions. A good example of this might be a promotion for Mothers' Day or Black Friday Sales. There is very little point in heading straight to the promotion element (which very often involves discounting your product for the promotion period) without first having established your product firmly on the platform.

The first element is the most important. You must allow your product to gain genuine customer reviews. Five to ten high-ranking (5-star) reviews is a good start. Without reviews there is little point in spending retail media advertising dollars at all. It would be a waste of money.

After gaining positive reviews you should then speak to your marketplace buyer specialist team on the platform and formulate a strategy of advertising that will give you the most value for money. Your advertising dollars will buy you exposure to more people. It will enable your product to climb the ranks of the competitive product listings and gain a higher profile (more views).

It is only at this point that you should consider taking part in retail media promotions. By doing so now, you are giving your product maximum exposure on the marketplace and a tempting, discounted offer for a limited period. The customer that has searched the marketplace for your product and perhaps even saved it in their 'wish list' will take advantage (and has probably been waiting) for this moment to buy.

By working in this way, you are establishing credibility with your 5-star reviews, gaining exposure with your advertising dollars, and then converting that exposure into sales with your promotional spend.

I will end this chapter with a word of caution. You can see how the strategy of marketing and advertising has changed over the last 20 years. It is continually evolving, and you must stand back and look at how marketplace platforms make their money. In general, they do not buy in and hold stock like a traditional retailer when you are dealing with them on a dropship basis. It is you who is undertaking the warehousing and logistic responsibilities. It should therefore follow that you have a slightly higher percentage of the available profit to pay for those responsibilities. You should set your prices to them accordingly.

One of the ways that they are now looking to maximise their profit is by making money from retail media. Effectively they are charging you to get your product in front of more people on their platform. They are using algorithms which ensure your product is climbing higher in the listings. If you advertise, it will climb higher!

Traditionally you would have spent your advertising budget throwing a wide net over several media outlets. The objective would be to bring in interested consumers who would then follow a trail to a retailer to buy your product. Now, marketplace platforms are asking you to spend your budget specifically with them. Remember, if you are advertising solely on Amazon, this advertisement is having little or no impact on eBay or Wayfair.

Retail media spent within a marketplace can be extremely lucrative if planned and implemented correctly. It can also be very expensive, and your overall budget can be consumed very quickly on one platform. Make sure that you budget your finances carefully and allow enough money on every platform you commit to for it to be a success.

In summary:

- Concentrate on social media platforms that are relevant to your customers.
- Keep up with your company's social media accounts and campaigns.
- Use social media to support your resellers.
- Reviews for customer confidence, then advertising for exposure, then promotions for conversion.
- Budget wisely and review your results.

17

Be a Professional; You Don't Need Luck

Having decided on a career in sales, you now have some decisions to make. The biggest one is deciding what you want to sell. Whatever that answer may be, I would urge you to pick something that really interests you. A sales career which stems from a passion you have is far more likely to succeed than if you are selling something that bores you. Choose your product category and industry wisely. You need passion for it.

Once your career is underway, you may decide to specialise. Do you want to be a new business salesperson or an account manager to existing clients? Do you want to ply your trade locally or extend your horizons nationally or internationally? Do you want to specialise in one category of customer? Do you want to be an e-commerce specialist?

Whatever you decide, if you follow the Denham Method you will succeed. Keep reading, keep learning, regularly take a step back, and observe the landscape in which you are operating. Notice if anything has changed and amend your strategy regularly.

My sales career has taken me to the farthest reaches of the world, and I have become friends with hundreds of people throughout my career, both colleagues and customers. I have never once been out of work, and I have enjoyed every moment of my working life. I hope that the information in this book enables you to do the same.

I was extremely proud of the most recent salesperson I trained. She never knew that she could be a future sales star and the thought of being a salesperson had almost certainly never entered her mind. She went through a very intense few weeks of training, firstly in the basics of how a business works and what each department does. Who is responsible within a company for which decisions.

I then enrolled her in a general external sales course so she could see how other people go about the task. I then spent a few days with her going through the Denham Method: showing her what a sales cycle was, how that related to the buying cycle, how to move a customer seamlessly through each step to complete the objective, and providing the customer with the best solution you have to solve their problem at the best possible price.

She was then assigned to work with a very senior salesperson who was responsible for our biggest accounts globally. She was asked to assist with the everyday tasks such as uploading product information onto marketplace platforms and ensuring that details were correct. I asked her to watch and learn and in maybe two years we could start to give her some accounts of her own to manage.

Within a year she was managing eight major accounts on her own and she had brought in four major (multimillion dollar potential) new customers to the business. Was there a secret to her success? No. She had a work ethic, she followed the Denham Method, she learned extremely fast, and she read the first draft of this book! She will go on to have an exceptional career in sales and will forever be in demand by any company who needs to generate revenue.

When we parted company, the last thing I said to her was 'I am not going to wish you luck because you don't need it. You have every tool to go forward now and be the most successful person you want to be.'

And that is the message I would like to leave with you: go forward and be the successful person you are meant to be.

18

The Denham Method: Summary

1. Research your territory and your potential customers.
2. Decide how much you want to earn, and reverse engineer your targets accordingly.
3. Use this to forecast in real time, and fix a forecast every month.
4. Maximise your prime selling time to achieve these targets.
5. Identify and follow the buying cycle, as well as the sales cycle.
6. Maintain control of the process through both cycles, and close every 'little sale'.
7. Review your business and personal targets regularly.
8. Ask for the order!

Section Two — Exporting (International Sales)

In recent years I was invited to sit on the Board, and eventually become Chairman, of Gardenex (the Trade Association representing British garden product manufacturers and exporters). The reason for this was that in my last business we were extremely successful in exporting our products around the world.

The truth is, we had no choice but to consider exporting as our main product was a seasonal selling item and if we did not export, then we would not have any sales revenue for 6 months of the year. The 'grow your own' sector in the UK makes the bulk of its sales from February through July. After that we had to chase the sun around the world. We had to export.

You or your company may have other reasons to export. If you have suppliers abroad and pay your bills in US Dollars, then you might want to generate some sales in US Dollars in order to naturally hedge the business against foreign currency exchange fluctuations. It may be that your product is ideally suited to another market and there is an opportunity there that gives you an advantage.

Whatever the reason may be, you need to plan your international sales business with solid research and an understanding of the costs involved in making it happen. There are numerous government initiatives that will help you to plan your strategy. In the UK your first port of call should be to the Department of Business and Trade (formerly the Department for International Trade or DIT). There are numerous links on their website to direct you to finding finance and support for your business.

In the early stages you should explore grants to expand your territory. There is an incredible amount of help and information available through grant export support teams. You will need to identify the size of the market, the competition, who the main players are, and the different business models in operation, as they may operate differently than domestic markets.

Once your research has been done and you have identified a suitable market you want to penetrate then you must carefully cost and plan your strategy to reach that market. Selling internationally is not an easy process. By definition, the distances are long and getting to see your customers is expensive. Every trip will likely involve a costly plane fare as well as hotel and food costs. Starting with an exhibition that serves customers in the proposed territory is a good start and there are match-funded grants available for first time exporters. However, you must plan to attend the chosen exhibition for several years to build up your reputation and prove to those international buyers that you are serious and in the game for the long haul, not just to make a quick buck.

The advantage of export business is that usually you are dealing with larger players and your orders will be relatively larger. It is uneconomical to ship a pallet of products to Australia or the USA, but far more reasonable when you are selling in container volumes. So, although your costs are larger so are your order values and profits.

My favourite overseas market, for my UK businesses, was the USA. I simply love selling to Americans. They speak English, they are relatively close to the UK, and the market is huge. They are not afraid of the word 'profit' and they expect everyone involved in the deal to make money. They also understand the buying process far better than other nationalities. That said, it is not an easy market to crack. You must have the right product at the right price and, if you are not professional in your approach, you will be found out very quickly.

I liken sales in America to British bands who try to make it there. It is extraordinarily hard work, but, if you make it the rewards are immense. Think Beatles or Rolling Stones as opposed to The Kinks or The Jam. I have seen many companies try to make it in the USA and fail.

As an example, it took my sales team some 5 years to break into QVC America, but we built the relationship to a point where we were offered a 'Today's Special Value' (TSV) slot on the channel. We put up a single product which retailed for $99 and we sold more than $3m worth of product in one single day. When I tell this story, people think 'oh wow, that's easy profit for a single day's work. They forget the hard work over the previous 5 years that it took to get us there.

If you are aiming for the US market, depending on your product, I would urge you to research it extremely well before you start and then, research State to State. Selling to California is very different than selling to Vermont. Whatever market you go for, if you do decide that you would like to specialise in international sales, please take the time to enjoy it and savour the places you visit. As a working salesperson I tried to take an extra day or a weekend if I was visiting somewhere new. It's not a holiday, but rather taking advantage of being there and immersing yourself in the local culture. It will help with your customers and your understanding of them. Other than that, the sales process and principles are the same. Stick to the Denham Method. Step your customer through the sales cycle and you will succeed. Be patient.

What specific skills do you need, to be successful in international sales?

An Understanding of the Market and Cultural Differences

As you will see from my 'sales tales', you need to understand the people you are selling to and their culture. You need to read their history, their traditions, and their values. Selling to a Sheik in Dubai is very different to selling to a Costco buyer in Seattle!

The Ability to Produce Your Product for That Market

By definition, the volumes for international sales need to be larger than your domestic sales in order to be viable. You need to ensure that your company can meet the demands of bigger orders and fulfil them in a timely manner. It is no good landing a deal to supply Home Depot in America and then realising that you are not able to meet their volume requirements.

Does your product comply with the legal requirements of the international territory? Do you have packaging and instructions in the correct language? Make sure these things are done before you start.

Solid, Realistic Objectives for the Territory, and a Realistic Timeframe to Reach Them

Do not try to achieve too much too soon. Be realistic. A buyer will not lose their job if they do not buy from you, but wait a year to see if you are having any success before they jump in with you.

Well-Researched Logistics

Delivering your products internationally is of course different to delivering domestically. Your company must research the market territory, including how you are going to ship and possibly warehouse your products (if that is necessary). Partner with a knowledgeable freight forwarder who has experience in the markets you are targeting. Make sure you understand the process and the costs involved.

Budget

You need to raise a business plan within your overall business plan for international sales. The costs are different, the margins are almost certainly different and the cost of getting a prospect 'into pipeline' is way more expensive. Your sales cycle will be longer than domestic customers and the longer it is, the higher your costs will be. If you are planning a foray into international sales you must have the backing of your management and a solid budget behind you that accounts for these considerations.

Your Personal Commitment

International sales may seem glamorous. The reality is that on a tightly planned overseas business trip you are likely to see an airport terminal, the inside of an Uber, a drab hotel room with room service and a customer meeting room. To maximise your time in a territory you may be going from one prospect to another and see virtually nothing of the country you are visiting.

It's also true that you will be away from home a lot. This suits some people more than others, but I would urge you to be honest with yourself before taking an international sales job on. Can you really be away from home for weeks at a time?

The Ability to Sleep Anywhere!

It sounds glib, but it is true. International travel on a regular basis is exhausting. You will find yourself waking up and wondering which city you're in today! Jet lag is a real thing and waking up in the middle of the night then not being able to go back to sleep is painful for your mind and body. You will need to train yourself to sleep when you can.

Some Basic Knowledge of the Local Language

Business is mostly carried out in English around the world, but if you learn some basic words and phrases in the local language, it will get you far. The minimum, 'hello', 'goodbye', 'please', and 'thank you' are essential. If you are fluent in a foreign language that is spoken in your target territory you will have a major advantage.

The Backing of Your Trade Association

Every industry has an associated Trade Association. Find yours and join if it is appropriate. They are usually staffed by people who have many years within your industry, and they tend to have 'been there and done that'. Their advice and contacts are usually second to none and they will often guide you on a particular territory and potential customers within that territory. They will often have 'meet the buyer' events which you can attend to meet overseas buyers visiting the association. This, in itself, is worth the cost of membership. Trade Associations are often also the gatekeepers for government funding of overseas exhibitions and conferences.

Section Three — Sales Tales

I have had some incredible experiences and met some amazing people on my travels as a salesperson. Here are some highlights and lessons!

Bad Buyers versus Good Buyers

I have to say that I have met some wonderful people throughout my career and most of the time we have done great business, which has been beneficial to both parties. In my last business we had a rule which said that we would only do business with people we liked and who were fair and professional in the way they did business.

Unfortunately, that rule had to be stretched as we started to deal with one of the biggest retailers in our marketplace (the garden industry). We had reached a size where we had to sell into one of the major garden centre chains to grow our UK business. At the time they had more than 30% of the UK market share.

The buyer for this garden centre chain was very clearly full of his own self-importance and very much enjoyed the power that he felt he had over visiting salespeople. One of his favourite tricks was to keep the salesperson waiting for up to an hour before seeing them. I found this infuriating and very unprofessional. The message from the buyer was, 'my time is more important than yours,' and he somehow felt that this gave him a negotiating advantage.

After this happened more than once and seemed to be an ongoing tactic of the buyer, I started the next meeting with 'timekeeping' as the first item on the agenda. I politely pointed out how far we were coming to see them and that our time is as valuable as his. I did not go as far as saying that I felt he was being rude and unprofessional, but the message was clear. Do not allow yourself to be bullied by any buyer or businessperson no matter how 'big' their status in the marketplace is.

Another tactic he used was to ask for a quotation on certain product lines, then ask for another quotation with amended (higher) volumes or a different mix of products, and then a further quotation with direct container volumes. He would then use these numbers to try to buy the smallest volume with the highest discount rate, not accepting the higher costs we would have in delivering smaller volumes. He did his utmost to create confusion across multiple quotations for multiple products.

Salespeople that are desperate to get their products into a large retailer like this will give in to the buyer's demands and sell at a price that will ultimately be unprofitable. My answer in this scenario is always the same: 'If you want me as a supplier to be here next year with new and exciting products, then we must make a profit. If we cannot come to an agreement that is fair and equitable for both businesses, then we will part ways.'

Business must be 'fair and equitable' for both parties. Like any relationship, if it becomes one sided then, at some point, one of the people will leave. When dealing with a company that is way bigger than you be careful that you stand your ground and ensure you are making a profit. Do not allow any buyer to bully you into making a deal that is unfair or unprofitable.

Another 'bad buyer' example is the one that will not see you under any circumstances. If you genuinely have a product that is new, innovative and well-priced, then it is that buyer's job to hear you out and consider your proposal. It is always hard work for you to reach the correct buyer in a major retailer and to get them to agree to an appointment. However, if they consistently put you off without a real reason for doing so then this is unacceptable. We are all busy people, but it is their job to see you and evaluate what you have to offer.

I have resorted to calling the Managing Director of their company and asking if I can come to see them to show them my products. When they ask why we haven't been through their normal procurement procedure, I am happy to tell them that the buyer does not have time to see me. Usually, they will see you or make the appointment with the buyer on your behalf. If you genuinely have a product that deserves to be seen, get that appointment!

I had another bad experience with a buyer at a global retailer who had buying offices across the world. I was quoting for delivery of products into the UK, and he insisted on comparing my quotation with the prices for which his Asian office purchased the product. Of course, he was not comparing 'apples for apples', and product supplied in Asia is a different specification and has different delivery costs. He refused to accept this reasonable explanation of any price difference (which was quite genuine), and dug his heels in to get a lower price based on his unfair analysis of the supply chain. In this instance, I had to walk away from the deal without hesitation. Two years later the buyer had moved on and we did superb business with the company dealing with a more reasonable buyer who had replaced him. Sometimes, you simply must wait them out!

The examples above of 'bad buyers' are very rare, but you will encounter them in your career. Have patience and never close the door to the buyer if you must walk away from one deal. Remember, it's a numbers game and your opportunities with that prospect will come again.

Over the years I have met with some superb buyers. People who know their job well, have a superb understanding of their customer base and demographic. They know what their customers' needs are and therefore, what their customers will buy. When you are sitting across the desk from them make sure you listen and learn from their experience. A good buyer in a major retailer will teach you more about your market than you can possibly learn elsewhere.

Remember when you are dealing with a major e-commerce company that there is a whole team and massive resources within that company to help you as a supplier. It's very easy to forget this as you are consistently interacting with a faceless portal and seemingly never speaking to an actual person. If you need help or advice from these companies, then push for it. They will respond and help you and their help will be invaluable.

You are a professional salesperson. You are doing a professional job on behalf of your company. It is the buyer's job to meet you with equal professionalism and respect. Any agreement you reach should be fair and profitable for both of you. If you enter the negotiation with this in the forefront of your mind, then you will succeed.

Interview with a Legend

Many years ago, I was working as a salesperson for the data communications division of a national telecoms company. My line manager was the head of the components division of the same company. Unfortunately, the manager did not have a sales background but was more technical in his expertise. I had arranged for a new salesperson to be interviewed and my manager insisted on conducting the interview.

The candidate was a very experienced salesperson who I had known for many years. He had a long and successful career in sales behind him and in my opinion was just what we needed to build the division going forwards.

The hiring manager thought he would ask a clever question to open the interview. There was a very large crystal ashtray on the managers desk, and he asked the candidate to 'sell me that ashtray'. I winced. It was a little degrading for the mature candidate to be asked to demonstrate his sales ability in this way.

Quick as a flash the candidate picked up the ashtray and threw it into the rubbish bin in the corner of the room where it smashed into a thousand pieces.

'You need a new ashtray,' he said.

Every sale starts with a problem...

Don't Leave Home without It!

In the 1990s I spent a few years in The Sultanate of Oman and The United Arab Emirates as a salesperson and had some amazing experiences throughout my time in the Middle East. At that time, I had a business selling online training packages to major corporations with the average sale value in the high hundreds of thousands of dollars and some creeping into the millions of dollars.

My first sales meeting in Dubai was a visit to Das Island LNG Terminal (just off the coast of Abu Dhabi), which I visited with a colleague the day after arriving. You would normally get the ferry over to the island with all the other visiting businesspeople, but we were late, so my colleague arranged for a speed boat to take us across. We passed the ferry with around 100 visitors to the island and were first to the dock as the ferry pulled in behind us.

As we arrived at security they asked for our passports and, of course, I did not have mine with me. There was a lot of discussion as to whether I could enter the complex and the queue of people behind were getting a little unsettled as they were waiting in full 35 Celsius sun! The only thing I had was my American Express card which they agreed to keep as surety until I left. As I walked sheepishly past the queue of mainly Americans waiting to pass security, one voice shouted, 'Don't leave home without it buddy!' I had managed to enter a highly secure Liquid Natural Gas terminal with a charge card!

Understanding Cultural Differences

One of the largest prospects I had at this time was one of the biggest companies in the world who happened to be based in

India. My sales cycle for this deal was to be (in the end) two years, but the deal was worth more than $13m.

Towards the end of the sales cycle, I was finding it very difficult to get the deal over the line. I was constantly being frustrated with excuses and objections that delayed any progress. I had promised (with the agreement of the customer) that the deal would close by the end of a particular quarter, and I quickly realised that this was not going to happen because of the delays imposed by the customer.

I was travelling between Dubai and India virtually every week to progress the sale, and just could not understand the delays being put in front of me. One of my Indian colleagues who was travelling with me at this time asked if I would like to have a day off and go and see the famous Elephant Caves which have been designated as a UNESCO World Heritage Site. I agreed, as it was a good opportunity to get out of the smog and humidity of the city for a day.

We arrived at a village and the Elephant Caves were incredible. Sculpted caves and temples that are simply beautiful and very spiritual. As we walked into the village centre, there was a man sitting cross legged on the dirt floor with his arm raised above his head and his arm was withered. My colleague explained that this was the man's way of devoting himself to God and that he had been sitting here like this for more than 20 years. The villagers brought him bread and water every day.

It suddenly dawned on me why my deal was stalling. I was pushing to get the deal closed within a very specific timeframe because my company needed that deal delivered for their financial reports. The customer, however, looks at these things in a very different way. They were in no hurry and had no timeline to meet. Their view of 'time' was vastly different from mine. If the deal took 3 months or 3 years, what would be would be, and I simply had not considered their viewpoint or indeed, understood their culture.

I immediately took a different approach. I chilled out. I enjoyed the customer interaction and built a more solid relationship. I stopped pushing for a decision. I let the customer buy when they were comfortable to do so. I told my managers to stop applying pressure to me and the customer. The deal would happen in good time. The deal was duly closed within a few months.

Whilst I was in India I bought a lot of books on Hinduism, Buddhism, and the teachings of the Dalai Lama. I would urge you to do so too. A salesperson at this level is under extraordinary pressure to deliver. You need to learn to relax and ground yourself to cope with this pressure.

Understand and allow for the culture of the people and company you are selling to. Remember that they are going through a buying cycle. The sales and buying cycle are measured in time and their definition of time may be different to yours.

Friends in High Places

During my time in Dubai in the mid to late 90's, I was travelling every week around the Middle East. I quickly gained 'Gold' traveller status and knew many of the Emirates Stewardesses by name. In 1997 alone I had almost 90 outbound flights from Dubai. It's fair to say, I was a seasoned traveller!

I had to travel from Dubai to Tel Aviv in Israel to see a prospective customer. Now usually you would have to fly to a politically neutral country and then catch a flight to Israel. The closest connection was via Cyprus which was a very long way. You had to take other precautions as well, such as using a second passport to ensure that you did not have an Israeli stamp in your main passport. This would have given me many problems if I then tried to travel to other Middle Eastern countries.

Emirates then introduced a flight via Cairo in Egypt which was much faster, so I decided to give this route a try. I flew the first leg to Cairo with no issues and made my way off the plane and towards the 'transit' area of the airport ready to catch my connecting flight. As I entered the transit area, I passed some very severe looking military men who were armed to the teeth and found myself in a windowless room with benches to each wall. There was one exit which went up some stairs and into the departure area. I was greeted by an Egyptian immigration official in military uniform and told to take a seat. He took my passport and disappeared up the stairs.

I sat and waited. Nobody came back to the room, and I was alone. I had 2 hours to my connecting flight departure to Tel Aviv and after an hour I started to get concerned. After an hour and a half, I was very concerned that I would miss my flight, so I made my way up the stairs towards the departure lounge. The Colonel's office was walled by glass, and I noticed he pushed my passport under his desk blotter as he saw me. He came out and stood in front of me. The Colonel was a large and imposing man with a huge moustache.

'Where do you think you are going?'

I greeted him in Arabic, and then in English, and explained that I was likely to miss my flight, so I would need my passport back before making my way to the gate. He denied having my passport and so I pointed out that it was under his desk blotter. He retrieved it and then accused me of having a fake passport. He nodded to a very young soldier standing to the entrance of the departure lounge who immediately drew his pistol and held the barrel to my temple.

Looking back, my reaction was extremely British. I put my hands in the air to show that I was no threat and asked him to call the British embassy immediately. I also asked if the safety catch was on!

As this was happening an Emirates Stewardess was walking past in the departure lounge and glanced across. 'Hi Joe, are you OK?'

'Morning! I have to say I have had better days.'

She immediately ran to the Emirates office and brought a senior manager to vouch for me and help me. The Colonel relented and let me go to catch my connecting flight after assurances from the Emirates staff that I was who I said I was. In truth, the Colonel was just playing with me. He knew I was flying to Israel, and, coming from an Arab country with a UAE residents permit in my passport, flying to Israel he had decided to give me a hard time. I arrived in Tel Aviv on time and had a wonderful visit. I also changed my return flights to route via Cyprus!

A Very British Dinner

My time in The Sultanate of Oman was incredibly special. I was headhunted to work for Sheik Salam Al Araimi in his trading company and I set up 3 trading divisions for him in Information Technology, Medical Products and Electronic Components. After two years the businesses were thriving, and I left to return to Dubai to start my own business.

Before I left, the Sheik kindly invited me to his house for a dinner in my honour with around 20 colleagues from the company. As I arrived with my wife to this incredible white-walled villa, we walked through landscaped grounds to the huge ornate wooden door which was open already. We walked into the most beautiful reception room which was octagonal with an Italian marble and gold staircase dominating the room. The right-side wall of the room was glass, and, behind it, there was a full-sized Dhow (traditional Omani trading ship) floating in water, making a spectacular display.

There was nobody to greet us in the hallway, so we followed the sweet smell of frankincense through the ground floor of the villa to the Sheik's reception room where he was seated with his daughters either side of him. After our colleagues arrived, one wall of the room was slid back to reveal a dining room decorated with Italian artefacts and dominated by a stunning wooden dining table. The meal started with smoked salmon flown in from Scotland especially for the occasion, followed by traditional roast beef with all the trimmings.

What an honour! What a wonderful and interesting man. It was an experience that I will never forget.

Friends in Low-Flying Places

One of my customers in Oman was the Oman Royal Air Force and I was dealing with an Omani Officer who was a Wing Commander and effectively the 'Number Two' in the ORAF. A lovely man who spoke fluent English and was educated at Oxford, he invited me and my wife to the Officer's Mess for a dinner.

Now we did not know that women guests were not usually allowed in the Mess, and we arrived for the dinner as honoured guests. The Omani pilots we were sitting with had not been expecting us and so we were somewhat of a curiosity. The evening went incredibly well, and I have never seen alcohol consumed in the quantity that was being downed that night. The finale of the evening was to be entertained by several traditional belly dancers!

This was 1994 and the first Gulf War was recently over (1990–91), so tensions in the region were still at a high. We learned that the pilots we were drinking with were on operations the next day, many practising low level flying over the Empty Quarter deserts of central Oman. We experienced incredible hospitality and were honoured to be sharing a meal with incredibly talented pilots.

I remember thinking that my sales career had granted me some amazing experiences, but this was surely a highlight!

Dragons' Den (in the Shark Tank)

My business partner and I were invited to appear on the TV program Dragons' Den (known as Shark Tank in the USA) when our business was just 10 months old. The VegTrug product was still new as a brand, and we were growing fast. We did the filming, but never appeared in the program as one of the Dragons was sick and try as they might, they could not edit around his absence.

Going through the process was interesting. I had spoken publicly to audiences of hundreds and never got nervous. On this day though, with a potential audience of 8 million, I was a little tense. We asked for too much money for a small percentage of our business and the reality was we never wanted the investment, just the publicity. One by one the Dragons fell away but by far the most positive was Theo Paphitis, who urged us to 'keep going'. By the end of our time in the Den he understood the product and the potential, but he had already declared himself out.

It would have been a great investment for them. We sold the business in less than 2 years after our appearance which meant they would have made 10 times their investment in that period.

One lovely footnote to this episode in my career was that some 4 or 5 years later we started to sell our products through the UK retailer Robert Dyas, which is owned by Theo. I messaged him to say that, for the value of their first order with us, he could have bought 30% of the company!

VegTrug is truly one of the businesses that was a Dragons Den missed opportunity.

Costco Stick Man

My Global Sales Manager and myself had a meeting at Costco HQ in Seattle a few years ago. It was a first meeting to introduce ourselves to the main category buyer for our products. Costco is the third largest retailer in the world. This was a big deal. We were shown into a board room to prepare for the meeting. It was a stunning room with an outlook from a full glass window to a central grass landscaped area that the whole company looked upon.

We looked out in awe of the company and the number of buildings and offices we could see; we prepared our presentation and then we sat quietly for a while. Then we got bored waiting. My colleague hopped up onto the board table and struck a pose for me to start drawing him. I was deep in artistic contemplation when the Senior Category Manager followed by her clipboard wielding entourage walked into the room. I put my finger to my lips to ask her to wait whilst I finished the drawing with a flourish. I then turned my pad around to show her my masterpiece whilst my colleague slid off the table and into a chair.

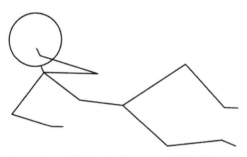

Costco Stickman © 2024 J Denham

She burst into hysterical laughter. Her colleagues followed suit after the initial look of shock at the scene they had walked into.

'I've seen some great opening introductions, but that is the best by far. You guys are crazy!'

Whenever we saw her at an exhibition or event, she remembered us. We did great business with Costco around the world. Make an impact. Never be forgotten.

Vous Êtes Foux

Having sold my company and retired in the early 2000s, my wife and I decided to move to France and buy a small (120 acre) farm in central Brittany. It is a beautiful part of the world and business there is dominated by the agricultural sector. The intention was to create a 'lifestyle' business which simply covered our costs and gave us a greater work/life balance. Having purchased the farm, we were interviewed by the local Chambre d'Agricole[11] about what we would be growing there. We told them that we had a plan to produce small bale haylage for horses. They asked the size of the bale and how much we would sell it for. My answer was 20kg and each bale would sell for 10 Euros. Haylage is a fermented hay that is made with a special mix of grasses and then fermented inside plastic wrapping or a sealed bag. It is a very sweet smelling and tasting hay very suitable for horses and particularly performance horses. The Bretons had never heard of this before as they were used to producing hay and Silage (a fermented hay that is very acidic and not suitable for horses) in very large bales and then selling that very cheaply as cattle feed.

'Vous êtes foux' (you are crazy).

They laughed aloud at the mad Englishman in front of them who had absolutely no agricultural or farming experience whatsoever. What they failed to consider was that I did know how to sell, however! I started to contact horse studs and owners in France and beyond. I started 'feeding the pipeline'.

In our first season we replanted the grass on the farm and managed to produce 800 bales of haylage. The specialist equipment I had invested in was tested and proven.

'Vous êtes foux,' they cried. Oh how they laughed.

In our second year we produced 20,000 bales and sold every one. They stopped laughing.

---

1   *The Chambre d'Agricole is the local authority in charge of the local agricultural business. They funnel grants and funding to farmers as well as set quotas and prices for produce. They also own and run hundreds of shops selling feed and materials in rural France.

In our third year we could not cope with the demand, so I partnered with a UK farm, and we started importing the product from the UK. We made a deal with the Chambre d'Agricole and began selling our product through their stores. We became the largest supplier of haylage for horses in Europe at that time.

The Denham method, when applied correctly, will always succeed!

Mind Your Language

My company was exhibiting at the National Hardware Show in Las Vegas. The biggest event of the year for my industry, and this was our second year attending the show. In England we call an exhibition space a 'stand' and in America it is called a 'booth'. Just one of the small idiosyncrasies of the difference between American English and English.

I was walking through the exhibition halls and happened to meet the Head Buyer for Home Depot. She had an entourage of around 10–12 people hanging on her every word as she perused the exhibition. I managed to catch her eye and introduce myself.

'I have a wonderful stand in Hall 5, the British section. Some super products that I think would fit well with Home Depot's offerings. Could I invite you to see my stand later today?'

She giggled and confirmed she would 'come to see my stand'.

It was much later that I learned that the word 'stand' is American slang for 'erection'.

Celebrate the Wins

It is so important that you celebrate your wins as a salesperson, especially the big ones. In the early days of my last business, I can remember counting how many boxes (products) we had sold each week, then we started counting how many pallets were going out. Pretty soon we were counting the number of containers that were being delivered. It then reached a point when we couldn't count on one hand how many factories we were utilizing.

When a business is growing in this way it is very easy to keep pushing forward and never take time to stop and celebrate the victories.

The standout moments for me were when we hit sales of $1m in a single month, and that was swiftly followed by 'Million Dollar Monday' when a million dollars' worth of business came in in a single day.

Your rewards do not have to be super-expensive: a day out to a sporting event, driving some fast cars around a track, or a nice meal. Do something that will be memorable and celebrate your success.

Life as a salesperson can be tough and very pressurised. Make sure you celebrate your wins. Take the time out to say, 'well done'. If your company does not recognise your small victory, make sure that you recognise it yourself and reward yourself. If you used the Denham Method to get there, drop me a line and I'll raise a glass to you!

Making a Difference

In 2017 I was asked to present a case in Parliament for supporting the Tradeshow Access Programme (TAP) grants on behalf of British business. I was there in my capacity as Chairman of my company and Chairman of Gardenex, the trade association representing British garden manufacturers for export assistance.

Presenting to an audience of around 300 people made up of MPs and Government Ministers, I made an impassioned plea for the government to support British business by supporting and extending the Government TAP scheme. This programme enables start-ups and small businesses to claim financial assistance in the early years to attend overseas trade shows, often under the British trade banner. We used this programme in the very early years. It paid for a couple of flights to the USA to attend the major trade show there and, at this time, it was a real help to us. We would not have been able to afford to attend the show otherwise.

After, many MP's approached me to say how impressed they were with my speech and vowed to do everything possible to support small British business to export. In the years following we have experienced major global disruption and austerity measures. I do hope that Government looks at this matter with more emphasis in the coming years. Small businesses like mine, and thousands of others, are the backbone of our economy and deserve all the support they can get.

I mention this story here because in 2017 my father passed away. All I could think of after my speech was how proud he would have been to see me speaking in the Houses of Parliament. For me, it somehow represented the culmination of my career to that point. All I have ever been is a salesperson, but I was pretty good at it!

About the Author

Joe Denham has setup and grown four very successful businesses in his lifetime.

His first major business success was when he sold his computer based training business located in Dubai for $10m in 1997.

He then had his own TV Show on Sky Television in the UK (Ideal World – Shopping Channel) for 4 years and he owned and operated a farm in Brittany France where he produced horse haylage as a specialist crop.

In 2009 he founded VegTrug which is an innovative raised garden bed which people could use to grow their own vegetables at home. That business was sold in 2012 and Joe continued to run the business as CEO until 2023. In that time the VegTrug brand was established globally, and more than 1 million units were sold.

Joe Denham
www.joedenham.com

**BUSINESS
BOOKS**

Business Books

Business Books publishes practical guides
and insightful non-fiction for beginners and professionals.
Covering aspects from management skills, leadership and
organizational change to positive work environments, career
coaching and self-care for managers, our books are a valuable
addition to those working in the world of business.

15 Ways to Own Your Future
Take Control of Your Destiny in Business
and in Life
Michael Khouri
A 15-point blueprint for creating better collaboration,
enjoyment, and success in business and in life.
Paperback: 978-1-78535-300-0 ebook: 978-1-78535-301-7

The Common Excuses of the Comfortable Compromiser
Understanding Why People Oppose
Your Great Idea
Matt Crossman
Comfortable compromisers block the way of anyone trying to
change anything. This is your guide to their common excuses.
Paperback: 978-1-78099-595-3 ebook: 978-1-78099-596-0

The Failing Logic of Money
Duane Mullin
Money is wasteful and cruel, causes war, crime and
dysfunctional feudalism. Humankind needs happiness, peace
and abundance. So banish money and use technology and
knowledge to rid the world of war, crime and poverty.
Paperback: 978-1-84694-259-4 ebook: 978-1-84694-888-6

Mastering the Mommy Track
Juggling Career and Kids in Uncertain Times
Erin Flynn Jay
Mastering the Mommy Track tells the stories of everyday
working mothers, the challenges they
have faced, and lessons learned.
Paperback: 978-1-78099-123-8 ebook: 978-1-78099-124-5

Modern Day Selling
Unlocking Your Hidden Potential
Brian Barfield
Learn how to reconnect sales associates with customers
and unlock hidden sales potential.
Paperback: 978-1-78099-457-4 ebook: 978-1-78099-458-1

**The Most Creative, Escape the Ordinary,
Excel at Public Speaking Book Ever**
All the Help You Will Ever Need in Giving
a Speech
Philip Theibert
The 'everything you need to give an outstanding speech'
book, complete with original material
written by a professional speechwriter.
Paperback: 978-1-78099-672-1 ebook: 978-1-78099-673-8

On Business And For Pleasure
A Self-Study Workbook for Advanced Business English
Michael Berman
This workbook includes enjoyable challenges and has been
designed to help students with the English they need for work.
Paperback: 978-1-84694-304-1

Small Change, Big Deal
Money as if People Mattered
Jennifer Kavanagh
Money is about relationships: between individuals and
between communities. Small is still beautiful, as peer
lending model, microcredit, shows.

Readers of ebooks can buy or view any of these bestsellers
by clicking on the live link in the title. Most titles
are published in paperback and as an ebook.
Paperbacks are available in traditional bookshops.
Both print and ebook formats are available online.
Find more titles and sign up to our readers' newsletter at:
collectiveinkbusiness-books.com/
Facebook: facebook.com/CINonFiction/
Twitter: @CINonFiction